RV

CAMPING

in National Parks

Exploring America's
Most Beautiful Landscapes
on Wheels

ANDREW TROTT

Table of Contents

Introduction

The appeal of RV camping in national parks

Few activities are more enjoyable than RV camping in national parks when it comes to discovering America's natural splendor. RV camping in national parks offers a singular and amazing way to connect with nature and make lifelong memories by fusing the freedom and flexibility of RV travel with the breathtaking scenery of our nation's most famous natural treasures.

The ease and comfort of traveling in your own mobile home as well as the chance to see some of the most stunning and recognizable natural wonders in the world are just a few of the numerous benefits of RV camping in national parks. In this essay, we'll look at some of the main factors that make RV camping in national parks so well-liked and enjoyable.

RV camping in national parks, first and foremost, provides unmatched access to some of the most stunning natural environments in the nation. National parks provide a broad selection of scenery that are sure to steal your breath away, from the towering peaks of the Rocky Mountains to the sprawling deserts of Joshua Tree. National parks provide something for everyone, whether you're an expert hiker, a wildlife enthusiast, or just looking to unwind and take in the beauty of nature.

A distinctive opportunity to escape the rush of daily life and re-connect with nature is provided by RV camping in national parks. Finding calm moments in today's fast-paced, technologically advanced society can be challenging. However, when you camp in an RV in a national park, you have the chance to disconnect from the stresses of contemporary life and really experience the sights, sounds, and sensations of the outdoors. National parks provide an opportunity to slow down, relax, and refuel your batteries, whether you wake up to the sound of birds singing outside your RV or gaze up at a starry sky at night.

The sense of community that RVing in national parks can foster is another major draw. The opportunity to meet people who share your passion for the outdoors and adventure when RV camping in national parks is available whether you're traveling alone, with friends, or with your family. RV camping in national parks may be a fun and social experience, with opportunities for campfire conversation and advise on the best hiking routes and scenic drives.

RV camping in national parks can provide a sense of community and natural beauty, but it can also have a lot of practical advantages. One benefit of RV camping is that you can move at your own pace and according to your own schedule. RV camping allows you the freedom and flexibility to design the trip that's ideal for you, whether you want to spend a few days exploring a single national park or take a multi-week road trip to visit several parks.

Other types of camping or travel cannot compare to the luxury and ease of RV camping. With an RV, you have access to contemporary conveniences like a full kitchen, bathroom, and entertainment system in addition to your own private place for sleeping, eating, and relaxing. Families with young children may find this particularly enticing because they can enjoy the conveniences of home while still having the opportunity to go camping in a national park.

Of course, there are difficulties associated with RV camping in national parks. Campsites might be in high demand and may need bookings in advance, depending on the park and the season. Planning and preparation are also necessary for RV camping, from selecting the ideal RV for your needs to carrying the appropriate supplies and equipment. While camping in an RV might be somewhat comfortable and convenient, it's vital to keep in mind that you're still in a natural setting and should be ready for anything, from bad weather to wildlife encounters.

In summary, RV camping in national parks is a special and satisfying experience that gives visitors a chance to interact with nature, forge lifelong memories, and discover some of the most stunning and recognizable natural sites on earth. RV camping in national parks is a type of vacation that appeals to a wide spectrum of people and families due to the sense of community and social connections it may foster as well as the freedom and flexibility it affords.

It's crucial to plan ahead if you're thinking of taking your RV camping in a national park. Make sure to select the ideal RV for your needs, bring the necessary supplies and equipment, and reserve your campsites in advance to guarantee availability. Above all, keep in mind that when RVing in national parks, you must preserve the environment and adhere to all laws and regulations.

RV camping in national parks is ultimately a chance to get away from the pressures of regular life and take in the natural beauty of our land. RV camping in national parks is an experience you won't soon forget, whether you're seeking adventure, relaxation, or a chance to connect with nature.

The advantages of exploring America's most beautiful landscapes on wheels

There are a variety of approaches one can take in order to take in some of the most breathtaking scenery in the United States. It is possible to travel around the national parks and other natural treasures of our country on foot, by bicycle, or even by canoe or kayak. However, there is another method to explore the splendor of the natural landscapes of the United States, and it is one that offers its own set of distinct advantages: exploring on wheels.

Traveling by car is a popular choice among tourists due to the many advantages it provides, including the opportunity to camp in recreational vehicles (RVs) and take road excursions through some of the most scenic parts of the United States. In this article, we will discuss some of the primary advantages of traveling by motor vehicle across some of the most breathtaking landscapes in the United States. These advantages range from the freedom and flexibility that such travel affords to the fresh insights that may be gained.

The freedom and versatility that comes with traveling across some of the most breathtaking landscapes in the United States is one of the most significant advantages of doing it by car. Exploring on wheels gives you the freedom to go at your own pace and design your own schedule, regardless of whether you're doing it in a car, an RV, or some other type of vehicle. You have the option of remaining in one location for as long as you'd like or moving on to the next location whenever you feel prepared to do so. This kind of independence and flexibility can be especially enticing for tourists who want to explore areas that are off the main path or who want to take their time to really take in the beauty of a particular location.

In addition, traveling on wheels enables you to cover more land and view more sites than you would be able to if you were walking or using any other mode of transportation. You are able to experience a wide variety of landscapes and natural wonders in a relatively short length of time if you are able to move swiftly and easily between sites, which enables you to explore many national parks and other natural landmarks within the course of a single trip.

One of the primary advantages of traveling by car across some of the most breathtaking scenery in the United States is the opportunity to gain new viewpoints. Exploring on wheels gives you the opportunity to observe the natural beauty of our nation from perspectives that are new to you. This is true whether you are cruising along one of our country's many picturesque byways or stopped at a breathtaking overlook. From a vantage point high in the mountains, you may take in breathtaking vistas in every direction, or you can see local wildlife and birds without leaving the comfort of your RV. These fresh viewpoints have the potential to teach you how to enjoy the splendor of the natural world in innovative and engaging ways.

Wheeling around provides a level of comfort and convenience that cannot be matched by any other mode of transport and is therefore unrivaled. You have your own personal place in which to sleep, dine, and rest whether you travel in a car or an RV, and you also have access to modern conveniences such as a fully equipped kitchen, bathroom, and entertainment system. This might be especially appealing for families traveling with young children or for senior travelers who may prefer the conveniences of home while still being able to experience the excitement of traveling through some of the most stunning landscapes in the United States.

There are many positive emotional and psychological benefits associated with traveling by bicycle in addition to the many practical advantages that come with this mode of transportation. Being in the presence of breathtaking natural scenery may have a profoundly restorative and reassuring effect, lowering levels of stress and enhancing feelings of wellbeing. When you explore on wheels, you may help to make memories that will last a lifetime and establish ties with friends and family members as you all enjoy in the excitement and adventure of seeing the natural wonders of the United States together.

Traveling on wheels presents its fair share of obstacles, it goes without saying. There may be restrictions or regulations that you need to be aware of, and they may vary according to the type of vehicle you are driving and the places you are going to visit. In addition to this, you will need to organize your trip in advance and properly pack your belongings in order to guarantee that you will have everything you require for your trip. And despite the fact that wheeled exploration can provide a certain amount of comfort and convenience, it is essential to keep in mind that you are still going in a natural setting and should be ready for the unexpected. This includes being prepared for interactions with wildlife as well as adverse weather.

In conclusion, traveling by motor vehicle through some of the most breathtaking landscapes in the United States offers a variety of advantages that make it an enticing choice for a lot of different kinds of tourists. Exploring on wheels is a way to connect with nature and make memories that will last a lifetime since it provides freedom and flexibility of travel, as well as the opportunity to see things from a new perspective and experience emotional benefits. It is crucial to do research and prepare ahead if you are thinking of taking a journey to enjoy the natural splendor of the United States while traveling by motor vehicle. Be careful to select the suitable mode of transportation for your journey, have the necessary supplies, and always be ready for the unexpected. When traveling by vehicle through some of the most breathtaking landscapes in the United States, it is imperative that you, above all else, keep in mind the importance of preserving the natural environment and abiding by all applicable rules and regulations.

In the end, traveling over some of the most breathtaking landscapes in America in a motorized vehicle provides an opportunity to experience the awe-inspiring splendor of our natural world in a manner that is simultaneously thrilling and relaxing. Exploring on wheels provides a one-of-a-kind viewpoint, as well as the opportunity to connect with nature and make experiences that will last a lifetime. This is true whether you're vacationing in an RV or driving across the country in your own vehicle.

Overview of the e-book's content

People are becoming increasingly interested in exploring the great outdoors while still being able to take use of the comforts and conveniences of their very own home on wheels as RV camping becomes increasingly popular. And what could be a better way to do it than by traveling to some of the most stunning national parks in the United States?

This e-book, titled "RV Camping in National Parks: Exploring America's Most Beautiful Landscapes on Wheels," is a complete guide to RV camping in a variety of the country's most beautiful and well-known national parks. This e-book contains all you need to know to plan and enjoy the trip of a lifetime, regardless of whether you've camped in an RV before or whether this is your first big adventure.

This e-book is broken up into six primary sections, each of which focuses on a different facet of camping in RVs in national parks.

The "Introduction" chapter is the beginning of the book and serves as a foundation for the following chapters. It introduces readers to the many benefits of visiting some of America's most stunning landscapes while traveling in a recreational vehicle and discusses the allure of camping in national parks with RVs. In addition, an overview of the content of the e-book is presented in the beginning. This gives the reader with a better understanding of what they might be learning and finding throughout the course of the book.

If you are new to RV camping or just need a review on the fundamentals, the second part, "Getting Started with RV Camping," is an essential resource that you should consult. This section covers everything from deciding which recreational vehicle (RV) is best suited to your needs and preparing for your trip, to RV camping etiquette and the rules governing camping in national parks. This section will assist you in getting off to a good start and ensuring that your RV camping vacation is a success, regardless of whether you choose to rent or own your recreational vehicle (RV).

The most exciting part of this article, "Top National Parks for RV Camping," may be found in the third section. In this part of the guide, we'll take a look at some of the most beautiful and well-known national parks for RV camping. Some of these parks include Yellowstone National Park, Grand Canyon National Park, Yosemite National Park, Zion National Park, Rocky Mountain National Park, Acadia National Park, Great Smoky Mountains National Park, Glacier National Park, Joshua Tree National Park, and Arches National Park. The details of each park, such as its distinguishing characteristics, well-liked activities, and RV camping alternatives, are presented here.

The fourth segment is titled "Exploring America's Most Beautiful Landscapes on Wheels," and it provides viewers with information that is useful for planning an RV trip that includes visits to national parks. This area provides information on a wide variety of activities, such as paths for hiking and bicycling, scenic drives and overlooks, wildlife watching and birding, and aquatic activities like as kayaking and fishing. This section also provides photographic advice for capturing the breathtaking scenery of national parks, which will assist readers in creating memories that will last a lifetime of their time spent RV camping.

The fifth chapter is titled "Planning Your RV Camping Trip," and it is in this chapter that readers will learn how to successfully plan and carry out an RV camping trip. This part covers subjects such as creating a travel budget and finding ways to save money on your RV vacation, determining the best time of year to visit national parks, making reservations for RV campsites and organizing your schedule, and learning about safety precautions to take while camping in a recreational vehicle in a national park. This section will help you plan and enjoy a vacation to some of the most beautiful national parks in the United States, regardless of how experienced a traveler or camper you are.

The sixth and final part of this e-book is titled "Conclusion," and it concludes the whole thing by supplying a rundown of the advantages of RV camping in national parks as well as concluding thoughts and suggestions. This section also provides information for preparing your RV camping vacation, including connections to websites, apps, and other useful resources. These resources can be used to help you prepare for your trip.

To summarize, "RV Camping in National Parks: Exploring America's Most Beautiful Landscapes on Wheels" is an indispensable reference for anyone who enjoys RV camping and wants to experience some of the nation's most stunning and well-known national parks. This e-book has something for everyone, whether you're a fan of the outdoors, photography, or you're just seeking for a more new and exciting way to travel. You will be able to organize and execute your very own RV camping vacation with the help of the in-depth information, useful recommendations, and breathtaking photographs.

The reader will find extensive descriptions of national parks scattered throughout the e-book, providing information on the parks' histories, geographies, and popular activities. The e-book also includes details on several possibilities for camping with a recreational vehicle, such as amenities offered at campsites, associated fees, and instructions for making reservations. The rules and etiquette for RV camping in national parks will also be covered in this book, enabling readers to better appreciate the natural beauties of the United States of America while acting in a polite and responsible manner.

The practical guidance on how to organize and carry out an RV camping trip is perhaps the aspect of "RV Camping in National Parks: Exploring America's Most Beautiful Landscapes on Wheels" that is the most beneficial. The e-book provides readers with the information they need to make their RV camping vacation a success. Topics covered include everything from creating a budget and finding ways to save money on your trip to determining the best time of year to travel to national parks to making reservations for RV campgrounds and organizing your route.

It doesn't matter if you've camped in an RV before or if this is your first time venturing into the great outdoors; "RV Camping in National Parks: Exploring America's Most Beautiful Landscapes on Wheels" is an indispensable guide to RV camping in America's national parks. This e-book is guaranteed to inspire and guide you as you plan and carry out your very own remarkable RV camping experience thanks to the extensive information, helpful recommendations, and breathtaking photographs that it contains.

Chapter I

Learning the
Basics of RV Camping

Choosing the ideal RV for your requirements

When it comes to camping in national parks with a recreational vehicle, one of the most essential decisions you'll have to make is which RV is best suited to meet your requirements. If you choose the wrong recreational vehicle (RV), your vacation could become uncomfortable, inconvenient, and unpleasant; on the other hand, the right RV could make your journey convenient, fun, and comfortable. In this article, we will discuss some of the most important aspects to take into account when selecting an RV that is suitable for your requirements, such as the RV's size, kind, amenities, and features.

When searching for the ideal RV to fulfill your requirements, the first thing you should think about is the vehicle's size. RVs are available in a broad variety of sizes, ranging from compact camper vans with space for two people to big motorhomes with sleeping quarters for six or more people. Your comfort level behind the wheel of a larger vehicle, your budget, and the number of people in your party will all play a role in determining the size of the recreational vehicle (RV) that you purchase.

It's possible that a camper van or a compact travel trailer might be the best option for you, depending on the size of your group and your financial constraints. These recreational vehicles are simple to operate and manuever, and they are frequently less expensive than bigger RVs. They might also have access to campgrounds that are more secluded or difficult to get to.

If you plan to travel with a larger party or if you simply desire more space and conveniences, a larger recreational vehicle, such as a Class A or Class C motorhome, might be the best option for you. These motor homes provide a greater amount of space for sleeping, cooking, and relaxing, in addition to a variety of conveniences such as complete kitchens, baths, and entertainment systems. They may also be more comfortable for longer journeys or for travelers that appreciate having more space and experiencing luxury during their travels.

When selecting the best recreational vehicle (RV) for your requirements, the type of RV should be your second consideration. Recreational vehicles (RVs) are available in numerous different types, each of which has a unique set of benefits and drawbacks. The following are the most prevalent types of recreational vehicles:

Class A motorhomes are among the most sought-after recreational vehicles on the market. The most opulent and roomy form of recreational vehicle (RV) camping is provided by these enormous, bus-like vehicles, which can be constructed on either a dedicated RV chassis or a bus chassis. Class A motorhomes have a wide range of amenities, making them suitable for accommodating big families or groups of people. These amenities include full kitchens, baths, and numerous sleeping places. These automobiles have an abundant amount of storage capacity, making them the ideal choice for lengthy journeys or extended vacations in national parks.

Class B camper vans, on the other hand, are the most compact form of recreational vehicle and are constructed on the chassis of a van. These little vehicles take a minimalist approach to RV camping and are meant for travelers who wish to be able to park and camp in any location. They offer less amenities than traditional RVs. Class B camper vans are typically equipped with everything necessary for a pleasant camping trip, despite their compact size. This typically includes a small kitchenette in addition to a sleeping area. They are an excellent choice for lone travelers or couples who are interested in touring national parks but do not require the use of a huge RV.

Class C motorhomes are a type of motorhome that is built on a truck chassis and are considered to be a mid-size RV. They include a comfortable cab-over sleeping area, a fully equipped kitchen, and a bathroom, thereby striking a balance between luxury and convenience. Class C motorhomes are easier to operate and park than Class A RVs, making them an ideal choice for individuals traveling with smaller families or groups. They have a large capacity for storage, making them an excellent choice for journeys that are expected to last at least a few weeks.

Last but not least, camping in national parks with an RV using a travel trailer is a common practice. Towable recreational vehicles are available in a wide variety of lengths, widths, heights, and designs, ranging from compact pop-up trailers to massive fifth-wheel trailers. Travel trailers provide you the freedom to explore more isolated regions because they can be detached from your vehicle, but towing them requires a more powerful vehicle. Because they provide a large amount of living space in addition to utilities such as a kitchen, bathroom, and sleeping areas, they are an excellent choice for families or groups of friends.

When searching for the ideal recreational vehicle (RV) to fulfill your requirements, amenities and features should be your third priority. Recreational vehicles (RVs) are capable of providing occupants with a diverse selection of conveniences and facilities, including full kitchens, baths, entertainment systems, and outdoor living areas. Off-grid camping can be made easier with certain features that are available on some recreational vehicles, such as solar panels and generators built right in.

When thinking about the available amenities and features, it is necessary to take into consideration your individual requirements and inclinations. For instance, if you want to do a lot of cooking while you're on your RV trip, a full kitchen that includes a refrigerator, stove, and oven may be very necessary. If you are traveling with a group that includes children or adolescents, it is possible that an entertainment system or an outside living area will be necessary in order to keep everyone entertained and comfortable.

When selecting the best recreational vehicle (RV) for your requirements, there are a few other aspects to take into consideration in addition to the RV's size, category, and amenities. These are the following:

When it comes to selecting an RV, one of the most important considerations to make is the budget. There is a significant price range for recreational vehicles (RVs), which can range anywhere from a few thousand dollars for a used camper van to hundreds of thousands of dollars for a brand new Class A motorhome. When looking for an RV, it is essential to take into account not only your budget but also any additional charges, such as insurance, maintenance, and fees charged by campgrounds. It is essential to avoid going overboard on expenses during your RV vacation by first establishing a reasonable budget and then sticking to it.

The driver's skill should also be taken into consideration. Consider your level of comfort behind the wheel of larger vehicles as well as your previous driving experience if you intend to operate your RV on your own. It can be difficult to operate and park larger recreational vehicles such as Class A motorhomes, particularly in confined areas. It is essential to pick a recreational vehicle (RV) that you feel at ease driving, particularly if you want to spend a significant amount of time on the road.

When selecting an RV, one of the most significant considerations you should make is how long your vacation will be. If you are only going to be gone for a few days, a less luxurious and more compact recreational vehicle can be all you need. On the other hand, if you intend to travel a greater distance or spend a greater amount of time in your RV, you may find that a larger, more comfortable vehicle that features a greater number of amenities meets your needs better. Take into consideration how much time you will spend in your RV as well as the necessities you will require while you are there.

Last but not least, it is essential to give some thought to any rules or regulations that could be in effect at the campgrounds you have in mind to visit. It is vital to perform research in advance to verify that your recreational vehicle (RV) is a good fit for the campsite that you have selected because certain campsites may have size restrictions or need certain types of RVs. Checking to see whether any licenses or fees are necessary to camp in national parks and other public areas is another crucial step to take before setting up camp.

In conclusion, selecting the appropriate recreational vehicle (RV) for your requirements is a significant decision that has the potential to affect the level of comfort, convenience, and happiness you derive from your time spent RV camping. You may choose a recreational vehicle (RV) that satisfies your individual requirements and enables you to experience the splendor of America's natural landscapes in a state of utmost convenience and luxury by giving consideration to aspects such as the RV's size, kind, level of amenities, and price.

Preparing for your trip: what to pack and how to plan
Planning and getting ready for a camping vacation in a recreational vehicle in a national park needs meticulous attention to detail. When getting ready for your trip requires you to think about a lot of different things, such as determining what to pack and how to get there, as well as mapping out your route. In this article, we will discuss some of the most important actions that you can take to guarantee that you are well-prepared for the RV camping trip that you have planned.

The first thing you need to do to get ready for your vacation is to make a decision about what you're going to pack. When preparing for a trip in an RV, it is essential to strike a balance between the level of comfort and the amount of space available. When you go traditional camping, you have to lug all of your belongings around on your back. However, renting an RV allows you to travel in an atmosphere that is both roomy and comfy. Despite this, it is still vital to minimize the amount of stuff you carry with you and only bring what is absolutely necessary. The following are some important things to remember to bring for your RV trip:

When preparing for a vacation to go RV camping, it is essential to bring clothing that can be worn in a variety of climatic situations. Be sure to pack some warm layers for the nights when the temperature drops, rain gear in case it rains, and sturdy hiking shoes for when you go exploring outside. Do not forget to carry your swimwear, especially if you intend to go swimming or visit some hot springs.

Although many recreational vehicles come with bedding already installed, you may find it more comfortable to bring along your own bedding. If you want to ensure that you get a decent night's sleep, you should think about carrying sheets, blankets, and pillows.

It is possible that you will not find any kitchen supplies in your RV; this will determine whether or not you need to bring your own. Be sure to bring along the necessary cookware, including pots and pans, utensils, and dishes, so that you can prepare and enjoy meals while you are away.

It is essential to bring along a sufficient quantity of non-perishable food products and beverages for your RV camping vacation. These should be goods that can be readily stored in your RV. Be sure to bring some snacks with you on the trip, and load up on necessities like water, coffee, and tea before you leave.

Consider bringing along some novels, board games, card games, and other diversions so that you and your traveling companions may pass the time entertaining themselves during downtime. These things can be helpful for passing the time during lengthy stretches of driving or on rainy days when there are fewer opportunities to be active outside.

Be sure to pack all of the essential goods for your personal care and hygiene, such as toothbrushes, toothpaste, and soap, as well as any medications or medical supplies that you might require. Protect your skin from the harmful effects of the sun and insects by bringing along some sunscreen and insect repellent.

In conclusion, it is essential to ensure that you are prepared for any unforeseen circumstances by bringing along the necessary tools and emergency supplies. It is recommended that you bring along a basic tool kit, a tire repair kit, a first aid kit, a flashlight with additional batteries, and a kit for repairing flat tires.

Following the step in which you determine what to pack for your RV camping vacation, the next step in the preparation process is to plan your route. Planning your route in advance will help you save time, avoid being stuck in traffic, and ensure that you have enough time to see all of the attractions that you want to see along the way. When you are planning your route, you should take into consideration things like:

When you are arranging the route that you will take for your RV camping trip, the location of the campgrounds is one of the most crucial things to take into consideration. Choose campgrounds that are situated in close proximity to the sightseing destinations that are most important to you so that you can devote more of your time to really taking in the sighting opportunities. Do some research on the various camping options available in the national park, and pick the sites that best meet your requirements and preferences.

When choosing a route for your RV camping trip, it is necessary to give serious consideration to the driving distances and the amount of time that will be spent traveling. If you are going to be traveling with young children or dogs, you should schedule more frequent stops so that everyone can get the rest they need and remain comfortable. Take into consideration stopping for the night at various campgrounds or hotels along the route in order to break up long stretches of driving.

It is well known that the natural beauty of national parks is breathtaking, and one of the best ways to experience this beauty is through traveling along picturesque routes. Think about going the scenic route and taking in the sights of the mountains, canyons, and waterfalls along the way, as well as any other natural features. Do some research on the various beautiful drives offered within the national park, and select the routes that best suit your preferences and interests.

Be sure to schedule frequent stops for rest and breaks when you plan the itinerary for your RV camping trip. This will ensure that you and your traveling companions have enough time to get some much-needed sleep. Take advantage of opportunities to stretch your legs, visit the restroom, and take in the beauty as you stop at rest areas. Ensure that everyone on the journey is fueled and hydrated by bringing along some snacks, beverages, and other necessities in their travel bags.

Following the completion of your route planning, the following step is to book accommodations at a campground. It is essential to make your campground reservation as far in advance as humanly feasible for national parks, particularly during the high travel season, when campgrounds are likely to fill up quickly. When making reservations at a campground, some important considerations to keep in mind include the following:

When selecting a campground, one of the most essential considerations you should make is the amenities that are available at that campground. You should make sure that the facilities that each campground provides, such as water and power hookups, showers, and closeness to hiking trails, are enough for your needs before deciding which campground to stay at. It is important to do some research in advance to verify that the campground you select provides the services you desire, as the range of amenities provided by campgrounds might vary greatly.

It is crucial to be sure that your recreational vehicle (RV) will fit comfortably in the space that you choose while selecting a campground. When choosing your choice, it is important to take into account the dimensions of both your RV and the campsite. Some campgrounds provide sites that are more spacious to accommodate larger recreational vehicles, while others may impose size restrictions on the sites.

Pick a campground that offers a convenient location in close proximity to the tourist destinations you intend to visit. You will be able to make better use of your time and get more out of your RV camping trip if you do this. Do some research on the various camping options available within the national park, and pick one that is situated in the park's geographic center and provides convenient access to the sights and activities you are most interested in experiencing.

It is imperative that you read over the rules and regulations of the campground in advance to ensure that you are well-prepared and able to adhere to all of the laws and regulations. The restrictions that each campground adheres to regarding quiet hours, campfires, pet policies, and other topics might vary greatly from one location to the next. It is in your best interest to familiarize yourself with the policies and procedures in advance so that you can prevent any unpleasant surprises or infractions during your vacation.

There are a few more things you can do to be ready for an RV camping vacation in addition to packing, planning your itinerary, and making reservations at campgrounds. These are the three most important steps. These are the following:

It is essential that you perform a pre-trip inspection of your RV to identify and address any mechanical problems or maintenance requirements. Check that the electrical, plumbing, and heating, ventilation, and air conditioning systems are all operating properly before continuing. To ensure that your recreational vehicle is in good condition for your vacation, it is essential to inspect the tires, brakes, and any other safety features that it may have. You can assist ensure a safe and comfortable journey if you take these procedures before setting out.

Be sure to have all of the relevant documentation with you on your RV journey. This includes your driver's license, documents pertaining to your registration and insurance, as well as any permits or passes required by the national parks or campsites you intend to visit. If you are prepared for your journey with these documents, you can prevent any problems or delays that might occur along the way.

It is crucial to always have a well-stocked first aid kit on hand in case of unexpected circumstances. This kit should have essential items such as bandages, gauze, disinfectant, and pain medicines. This will ensure that you are ready to deal with any small injuries or illnesses that might crop up while you are on your trip.

Be sure to carry all of the necessary supplies for your pets, such as food, water, and bedding, if you intend to bring them on your RV journey with you. Researching ahead of time which campgrounds and national parks allow pets and ensuring that your pets' immunizations are up to date are two additional things that should be prioritized when planning a trip with your four-legged friends. If you follow these instructions, you will be able to make sure that your pets are secure and have a pleasant journey.

It is essential to maintain order when living in a confined area, such as an RV, in order to make the most of the space available and prevent clutter. Take into consideration the use of packing organizers, such as storage boxes and hanging organizers, in order to maintain the orderliness of your stuff. You will be able to make better use of the space you have, as well as maintain a clean and comfortable environment in your RV throughout your vacation.

In conclusion, it is necessary to do a lot of planning and preparation work before going on a camping vacation in a recreational vehicle in a national park. You can make sure that your RV camping trip is pleasant, safe, and fun by packing lightly, planning your route, making campground reservations, inspecting your RV, bringing vital paperwork, packing a first aid kit, arranging for pets, and being organized. You can make memories that will last a lifetime and enjoy the breathtaking natural landscapes of the United States in an original and thrilling way if you come prepared and have the correct frame of mind.

RV camping etiquette and regulations in national parks

Camping in a recreational vehicle within one of America's national parks is one of the best ways to experience the country's breathtaking natural scenery. To guarantee that you, your fellow campers, and the environment are respected and safeguarded at all times, it is essential to follow correct RV camping etiquette and rules. In this section, we will discuss some important RV camping etiquette and rules that you should be aware of when camping in national parks. These guidelines apply specifically to those camping in RVs.

The observance of quiet hours is considered to be one of the most essential components of proper RV camping etiquette. The majority of campgrounds within national parks have designated quiet hours, which normally range from 10 p.m. to 6 a.m. Campers should refrain from creating loud noises or playing loud music during these hours in order to minimize the potential for upsetting other campers. The observance of quiet hours helps to guarantee that everyone is able to have a night of sleep that is undisturbed and rejuvenating.

Putting the "Leave No Trace" ideas into action is another essential component of proper RV camping etiquette. This requires you to remove all garbage and rubbish from the campground and ensure that it is left in the same state of cleanliness as you found it. It is important to refrain from leaving behind any trash or objects that could be harmful to the local wildlife or the environment. Make sure to throw away any waste or garbage in the containers that have been designated for that purpose.

In order to limit the spread of wildfires, many national parks have implemented stringent fire bans. It is essential to constantly adhere to these rules and to never light a fire outside of the fire pits or rings that have been designated for that purpose. If you are unsure about the fire regulations in the region, you should approach the park rangers or the hosts of the campground for assistance.

Campgrounds in national parks typically have a set of laws and regulations in place to safeguard everyone's health and safety as well as their level of comfort. It is essential that you become well-versed in these guidelines and that you adhere to them at all times. Restrictions could be placed on the ownership of pets, the operation of generators, or the use of outdoor lighting. Before you set up camp at the campsite, be sure you have read and fully comprehended all of the laws and regulations.

Respect for these animals and the environments in which they live is essential, as national parks are home to a wide variety of different species of plants and animals. It is best to refrain from feeding wild animals as this may lead to them becoming reliant on human food and causing them to lose their natural instincts. In addition, it is essential to maintain a secure distance from wild animals and to absolutely never approach or make any kind of contact with them.

It is imperative that campers practice responsible behavior when making use of on-site amenities such as showers, restrooms, and water sources. It is important to refrain from wasting water and to keep the facilities from getting unclean or unsanitary. When utilizing these facilities, make sure to follow all of the printed guidelines and report any difficulties or complaints to the staff at the campground.

Etiquette for camping in an RV also includes showing consideration for other people who are staying at the campground. Playing loud music or generating other loud noises that could annoy other people should be avoided. It is important to respect the space and privacy of other campers and to refrain from going through their sites. If you own a pet, you have the responsibility of keeping it under control and cleaning up after it at all times.

There are special rules that must be followed in order to camp in a recreational vehicle in a national park, in addition to the RV camping etiquette that must be followed. These rules and regulations could be different depending on the campground and the park, however some of the most typical rules and regulations are as follows:

There are restrictions on the number of tents and recreational vehicles that can be set up at each campsite in most national park campgrounds. Be sure to adhere to these restrictions and avoid making your campsite too crowded at all costs. This will ensure that you and the other campers have a pleasant and comfortable experience overall.

There are regulations placed on the usage of generators in several national parks, particularly during quiet hours. Make sure that you are familiar with these restrictions, and that you only use your generator during the times that are designated. Because of this, it will be much easier for everyone at the campground to take advantage of the serene atmosphere of the great outdoors.

As was just discussed, many national parks are subject to stringent regulations regarding the use of open flames. It is essential to comply with these regulations and to light fires in fire pits or rings that have been specifically designated for that purpose. This will assist in the prevention of wildfires and will save the natural beauty of the park.

There may be limitations placed by some national parks on the sizes or types of motor vehicles that are permitted in campgrounds or on particular routes within the park. Be sure to check well in advance to see if bringing your RV into the park is permitted, and be sure to adhere to any and all vehicle restrictions. You will be able to navigate the park and its roads with greater ease and safety as a result of this.

The majority of campgrounds within national parks are equipped with disposal stations where recreational vehicles can dispose of their garbage. It is essential to adhere to all of the guidelines that have been set and to dispose of your garbage in an appropriate manner in order to avoid causing damage to the environment or to the other campers. This will contribute to maintaining a clean and secure environment for everyone who uses the park.

There are typically laws in place regarding pets in national parks, such as those requiring them to be on a leash and imposing boundaries on where they are permitted to go. It is imperative that you become well-versed in these rules and standards and that you adhere to them at all times. This will assist to ensure that your pet is protected and comfortable throughout your trip, as well as that you are respectful to the natural environment of the park in which you are visiting.

Camping in recreational vehicles may require permits or passes in many national parks, particularly in wilderness regions. Be sure to check in advance to see if any permits are necessary, and then make sure to secure them well in advance of your trip. This will help guarantee that you are prepared for your vacation and that you will be able to enjoy it without having to deal with any problems or delays.

You can help guarantee that you and your fellow campers have a camping experience that is safe, fun, and polite by adhering to the restrictions that are in place for RV camping in national parks and embracing the appropriate RV camping etiquette. To get the most out of your RV camping trip in a national park, it is essential to show consideration for your fellow campers, observe all of the park's rules and regulations, and show respect for the natural environment and the animals that call the park home.

Chapter II

Most Popular National Parks
for RV Camping

Yellowstone National Park

Yellowstone National Park is widely considered to be one of the most visited national parks in the United States due to the tremendous natural beauty that can be found there as well as the wide variety of animals that can be found there. Yellowstone National Park has more than two million acres, the most of which are located in Wyoming, but it also extends into Montana and Idaho. Each year, the park welcomes tens of millions of tourists.

Yellowstone was the first national park to be founded in the United States, and its creation in 1872 was motivated primarily by the desire to protect the extraordinary natural features of the park for future generations. In order to make room for the national park's establishment in the late 1800s, a significant number of Native American tribes were forcibly evacuated from the area. This chapter of the park's history is regarded as one of the most troubling in its whole.

Geysers, hot springs, and multicolored rock formations are just some of the geological attractions that can be found at Yellowstone National Park. Because the park is located on top of a big volcanic hot point, the ground there is always active and alive with geothermal activity. Old Faithful, a geyser that erupts at regular intervals, and the Grand Prismatic Spring, a massive hot spring famed for its bright colors, are two of the most notable geothermal features in the area. Both of these features are located in Yellowstone National area.

Yellowstone is also well-known for the abundance and variety of its native flora and fauna. The park is home to a number of well-known animal species, such as grizzly bears, wolves, bison, and elk, among other animals. The park is an essential habitat for these species as well as a great number of other species, and tourists frequently get the opportunity to witness wildlife up close either hiking through the park or driving through the park.

Yellowstone National Park is home to a vast array of sights and pursuits that guests can participate in during their time there. In addition to the geothermal features and opportunities for watching wildlife, visitors to the park can explore the various hiking routes in the park, go fishing or boating in one of the area's many lakes and rivers, or even do rock climbing or horseback riding. Additionally, there are a number of tourist centers and museums located within the park that provide information on the history, geology, and animals of the area.

The Grand Canyon of the Yellowstone is a large canyon with steep walls and a rushing river running through the bottom. It is one of the most popular attractions in the park and draws a lot of visitors every year. Visitors have a number of options for vantage points from which to observe the canyon, including walking around the rim or descending into the canyon on one of the many trails. Mammoth Hot Springs is another one of the area's well-known tourist destinations. It is a complex of hot springs and terraces that produce unearthly white, orange, and brown formations.

Visitors to Yellowstone National Park have the option of staying in one of the park's several lodges or campgrounds, or they can choose to stay in a town that is close by but is located outside the park itself. Visitors have a variety of alternatives to choose from when it comes to camping within the park, ranging from rustic campsites to RV sites that are equipped with full hookups.

It is imperative that park visitors keep in mind the laws and regulations that regulate visitor behavior while they are in the park. These rules include guidelines for interacting with wildlife, camping, and hiking in the park. The weather in the park is notoriously unstable, and visitors should come prepared for anything, including the possibility of snowfall even in the warmest months of the year.

In conclusion, Yellowstone National Park is a place that is genuinely extraordinary since it is packed with one-of-a-kind geological wonders, a broad range of species, and a rich history. There is something for everyone to do in Yellowstone, whether it's going on a hike, setting up a tent, or simply taking in the park's stunning sights. Visitors may assist in ensuring that this extraordinary natural marvel will continue to be protected and preserved for future generations to enjoy if they adhere to the park's rules and regulations and engage in responsible tourism practices while they are there.

Grand Canyon National Park

The Grand Canyon is one of the most famous and stunning natural wonders in the United States, and its national park bears its name. The enormous canyon at this park in Arizona extends for more than 277 miles in length, up to 18 miles in width, and more than a mile in depth. The park is located in the state of Arizona.

There is evidence of human habitation in the Grand Canyon that dates back more than 12,000 years. This area has a long and rich history. In the 16th century, Europeans conducted the first known exploration of the region; nonetheless, it wasn't until the late 1800s that the region was designated as a national monument. It wasn't until 1919 that the region was formally recognized as a national park, so assuring that it would be preserved for the benefit of future generations.

There are layers of rock formations in the Grand Canyon that depict the narrative of almost two billion years of Earth's history. This makes the Grand Canyon a geological wonder. The rocks that are visible in the walls of the canyon range in age from Precambrian rocks, which are the oldest, to more recent formations that were formed during the Paleozoic and Mesozoic eras, which are the most recent. Over the course of millions of years, the Colorado River formed the canyon by eroding the rock, which resulted in the formation of the precipitous cliffs and expansive canyon that we see today.

In addition to being home to a wide variety of plant and animal life, the Grand Canyon is also inhabited by a number of different kinds of mammals, birds, and reptiles. While touring the park, guests may have the opportunity to catch a glimpse of wildlife such as bighorn sheep, mule deer, and coyotes. The park is also home to a variety of species that are in risk of becoming extinct or are already extinct, such as the California condor and the humpback chub.

The Grand Canyon is home to a variety of sights and pursuits that guests can participate in during their time there. One of the most well-liked things to do is go hiking, and there are a variety of paths ranging in difficulty from very basic to quite severe. The Bright Angel Trail, the South Kaibab Trail, and the Rim Trail are some of the most well-known paths for hikers to take along the South Rim of the canyon, which is the most popular place to go hiking in the entire canyon.

The park features a number of scenic drives, such as the Desert View Drive and the Hermit Road, for those who would rather participate in a less physically demanding activity. In addition, guests can take a ranger-led tour of the park, go whitewater rafting or kayaking on the Colorado River, or participate in one of the other activities offered by the park.

In addition, the park is home to a number of historic buildings, one of which is the El Tovar Hotel, which was constructed in 1905 and is now recognized as a National Historic Landmark. The Kolb Studio, which was constructed in 1904 and is now a museum and gallery showing the artwork and photography of the Kolb brothers, is also available for guests to visit during their time in the city.

Visitors to Grand Canyon National Park have the option of staying in one of the park's lodges or campgrounds, or they can choose to stay in one of the surrounding communities that are not inside the park's boundaries. Tent and recreational vehicle camping are also permitted in the park's multiple campgrounds, making this activity a well-liked choice for visitors. Visitors to the park should come prepared for the high elevation and harsh temperatures that can be found there, which can range from temperatures below freezing in the winter to temperatures that are over 100 degrees Fahrenheit in the summer.

It is necessary for visitors to the park to respect the rules and regulations governing visitor behavior, which includes guidelines regarding encounters with wildlife, hiking safety, and camping requirements. The remote position of the park, with limited access to amenities and services in certain regions of the park, is another factor that visitors should be prepared for.

In conclusion, Grand Canyon National Park is a magnificent location that is known for its breathtaking scenery, one-of-a-kind geological attractions, and extensive history. There is something for everyone to do at the Grand Canyon; whether you want to go hiking, camping, or just take in the breathtaking scenery, the Grand Canyon offers it all.

Yosemite National Park

The Sierra Nevada mountain range in California is home to the beautiful Yosemite National Park, which is known as a natural wonder. It is famous for the towering granite cliffs, plunging waterfalls, and verdant valleys that can be found there.

At least 3,000 years of human occupancy can be traced back to the region that is now home to Yosemite National Park. This region has a rich history of human occupation. People who went by the name Ahwahneechee are credited with being the first known occupants of the area. For generations, they coexisted peacefully with the natural environment. Around the middle of the 19th century, European Americans started venturing into the area, with many of them deciding to make a permanent home there. By the late 1800s, Yosemite Valley had already established itself as a popular tourist attraction, and in 1890, the region was given the status of a national park.

Glaciers have worked over the course of millions of years to sculpt Yosemite National Park's breathtaking scenery. The park is situated on the western slopes of the Sierra Nevada mountain range. The most famous landmark in this national park is called Half Dome, and it is a gigantic granite dome that stands 8,842 feet above mean sea level. In addition, the park is home to a number of additional granite formations, the most notable of which being El Capitan and Cathedral Rocks. The Yosemite Valley, which can be found in the middle of the park, was formed by glaciers and is known for its precipitous cliffs and waterfalls that cascade down them.

There are several kinds of mammals, birds, and reptiles that call Yosemite National Park their home. This park is home to a broad diversity of wildlife. While exploring the park, guests may get a glimpse of a bighorn sheep, a black bear, or a mountain lion, depending on their level of luck. In addition, the park serves as a habitat for a number of species that are in risk of extinction, such as the Sierra Nevada bighorn sheep and the Yosemite toad.

Yosemite National Park is home to a wide variety of exciting experiences and sights for guests to enjoy during their time there. One of the most well-liked things to do is go hiking, and there are a variety of paths ranging in difficulty from very basic to quite severe. Hiking up the Mist Trail, which takes hikers to the top of both Vernal and Nevada Falls, is one of the most popular things to do in the area. In addition to Yosemite Falls and Bridalveil Fall, this national park is home to a number of other breathtaking waterfalls.

The park features a number of scenic drives, such as the Tioga Road and the Glacier Point Road, for those who would rather participate in a less physically demanding activity. In addition, guests can participate in activities such as rock climbing, bouldering, or one of the many programs that are offered by park rangers during their time at the park.

In addition, the park is home to a number of historic buildings, one of which being the Ahwahnee Hotel, which was constructed in 1927 and is now recognized as a National Historic Landmark. In addition, guests have the opportunity to investigate the Yosemite Valley Chapel, which was constructed in 1879 and is still in operation today.

Visitors to Yosemite National Park have the option of staying in one of the park's lodges or campgrounds, or they can choose to stay in one of the neighboring towns rather than inside the park itself. Tent and recreational vehicle camping are also permitted in the park's multiple campgrounds, making this activity a well-liked choice for visitors. Visitors to the park should come prepared for the high elevation and harsh temperatures that can be found there, which can range from temperatures below freezing in the winter to temperatures that are over 100 degrees Fahrenheit in the summer.

It is necessary for visitors to the park to respect the rules and regulations regulating visitor behavior, which includes guidelines regarding encounters with wildlife, hiking safety, and camping requirements. The remote position of the park, with limited access to amenities and services in certain regions of the park, is another factor that visitors should be prepared for.

In conclusion, Yosemite National Park is an extraordinary location that is known for its beautiful scenery, unique geological attractions, and extensive history. There is something for everyone to do at Yosemite, whether you want to go hiking, camping, or just take in the breathtaking scenery. Yosemite National Park is located in California. Visitors can aid in the protection of this natural marvel for future generations by abiding by the park's rules and regulations and engaging in responsible tourist practices while they are there.

Zion National Park

The breathtaking natural wonder that is Zion National Park can be found in the southwestern corner of Utah. This park is visited by tens of millions of people every year due to the impressive sandstone cliffs, canyons, and waterfalls that can be found inside its boundaries.

Zion National Park is home to a significant amount of human activity dating back more than 8,000 years. The Ancestral Puebloans were the first people to settle in the area. They built their dwellings and granaries in the canyons located throughout the park. Later, individuals who identified as Paiute moved into the region and began using the terrain for hunting and gathering.

In the late 1800s, European Americans started to explore the region, and shortly thereafter, it gained popularity as a location for artists and photographers to visit. The region was initially declared as a national monument by President William Howard Taft in 1909, and then it was converted into a national park the following year in 1919.

The breathtaking topography of Zion National Park is the result of geological processes like erosion, uplift, and faulting, which took place over the course of millions of years. The park's location in the transition zone between the Mojave Desert and the Colorado Plateau gives it a distinctive blend of desert and alpine habitats, making it one of the most popular national parks in the United States.

The towering sandstone cliffs are perhaps the most recognizable aspect of this national park. They soar up to a height of 2,000 feet above the canyon floor. The park is also home to a number of canyons, the most well-known of which being Zion Canyon, which stretches for 15 miles and may reach depths of up to half a mile.

There are several kinds of mammals, birds, and reptiles that call Zion National Park their home. This park is home to a broad diversity of wildlife. While exploring the park, guests might get a glimpse of a mule deer, bighorn sheep, or even a coyote if they're lucky. Additionally, the park is home to a number of species that are in danger of extinction, including the California condor and the Zion snail.

Visitors will find a wide variety of opportunities to engage in fun pursuits and exciting attractions throughout their time at Zion National Park. One of the most well-liked things to do is go hiking, and there are a variety of paths ranging in difficulty from very basic to quite severe. The park is home to a number of well-known hikes, one of which is called Angel's Landing. This hike is a challenging 5 miles long and rewards hikers with breathtaking views of the canyon.

The park 45eaturees a n'mber of scenic drives, including the Zion Canyon Scenic Drive and the Kolob Canyons Scenic Drive, for those who would rather participate in a less physically demanding activity. In addition, guests have the opportunity to take part in one of the several ranger-led activities or go on a guided tour of the park.

In addition, the park is home to a number of historic buildings, one of which is the Zion Lodge, which was constructed in 1925 and is now recognized as a National Historic Landmark. The park's ancient homesteads and cabins, which provide guests with an insight into the region's rich human past, are also available for exploration by guests.

Visitors to Zion National Park have the option of staying in one of the park's lodges or campgrounds, or they can choose to stay in one of the neighboring communities rather than inside the park itself. Tent and recreational vehicle camping are also permitted in the park's multiple campgrounds, making this activity a well-liked choice for visitors. Visitors to the park should come prepared for the high elevation as well as harsh temperatures that can be found there, which can range from temperatures below freezing in the winter to temperatures that are over 100 degrees Fahrenheit in the summer.

It is necessary for visitors to the park to respect the rules and regulations regulating visitor behavior, which includes guidelines regarding encounters with wildlife, hiking safety, and camping requirements. The remote position of the park, with limited access to amenities and services in certain regions of the park, is another factor that visitors should be prepared for.

In conclusion, Zion National Park is an amazing place to visit because it provides visitors with stunning views, one-of-a-kind geological wonders, and a deep human history. There is something for everyone to do at Zion, whether you want to go hiking, camping, or just take in the breathtaking scenery. Zion National Park is a place that all people who have a passion for nature should go at least once because it contains a wide variety of plants and animals, as well as historic buildings and scenic roads.

Rocky Mountain National Park

There is a solid reason why Rocky Mountain National Park is one of the most popular destinations within the country's network of national parks. The park covers an area of 415 square miles in Colorado and is home to unspoiled wilderness, including some of the highest peaks in the Rocky Mountains. Anyone who enjoys being outside should make it a point to go to Rocky Mountain National Park at least once because of the park's breathtaking scenery, abundant wildlife, and many opportunities for outdoor recreation.

Although Rocky Mountain National Park is most famous for its breathtaking mountain scenery, it is also home to a diverse collection of other natural attractions, including geological formations. A portion of the Front Range, a chain of mountains that runs from Colorado to Wyoming, can be found inside the park's boundaries. Longs Peak, which is the highest point in the park and is located at an elevation of 14,259 feet above mean sea level, is one of the most popular destinations for climbers and hikers.

In addition, a great number of lakes, rivers, and waterfalls may be found inside the park. Whitewater rafting and fishing along the Colorado River, which winds its way through the park, are two activities that draw a lot of visitors. In addition, there are over 150 lakes and a great number of waterfalls, the most well-known of which are the Alberta Falls and the breathtaking Ouzel Falls.

Elk, moose, bighorn sheep, mountain lions, and black bears are just few of the animals that call Rocky Mountain National Park their home. Other species include mountain lions and bighorn sheep. The park is notably well-known for its herd of elk, which may be seen grazing in the park's various meadows and along its roadways. This herd is the primary reason for the park's popularity. Birdwatchers flock to the park since it is home to more than 280 different species of birds, making it a desirable location overall.

Hiking, camping, fishing, horseback riding, and seeing animals are just some of the outdoor pursuits that may be enjoyed in Rocky Mountain National Park. There are over 350 miles of trails throughout the park, and they range from casual strolls to challenging climbs that entail climbing and scrambling over rocks and other obstacles. The trail that leads to Chasm Lake, the trip that goes to Sky Pond, and the climb that goes all the way to the top of Longs Peak are some of the most popular hikes in the park.

The park features a number of scenic drives, whichh are available for visitors who would rather participate in a more relaxed activity. The Trail Ridge Road is a drive that is 48 miles long and brings visitors above the tree line. Along the way, they are treated to breathtaking vistas of the park's alpine tundra and snow-capped peaks. The route brings tourists through a wide range of environments, from lowland grasslands and woodlands to highland tundra and ice fields.

Tent and recreational vehicle camping are both permitted in the park's multiple campgrounds, which contribute to the popularity of this pastime. Camping in the backcountry is also permitted, but requires a permission. One more well-liked pastime in the park is fishing, which can be done in any one of the many lakes, rivers, or streams that are present. The park is home to a number of different kinds of fish, the most notable of which are the brown, rainbow, and cutthroat trout.

There are a number of visitor centers and museums located within Rocky Mountain National Park. These centers and museums provide information about the history, geology, and wildlife of the park. The Beaver Meadows Visitor Center is the primary visitor center for the park and features exhibits on the natural and cultural history of the region. Additionally, the center provides information on hiking trails and camping areas. Both the Moraine Park Discovery Center and the Alpine Visitor Center both provide visitors with information and exhibits related to the natural history of the park.

It is imperative that visitors to Rocky Mountain National Park observe all of the rules and regulations that pertain to appropriate conduct within the park. Visitors are expected to show respect for the local species, refrain from approaching or feeding the animals, and bring appropriate clothing and gear for the park's secluded position and high temperatures. It is also essential to put the Leave No Trace principles into reality, which include removing all waste from the area and avoiding hurting the surrounding plants or rock formations.

In conclusion, Rocky Mountain National Park is a fantastic location that provides something of value to visitors of all ages and interests. Rocky Mountain National Park is a place that should not be missed by anyone who has even a passing interest in the great outdoors due to its breathtaking mountain scenery, abundant wildlife, and plenty of opportunities for outdoor recreation, as well as its various visitor centers. As a result of the park's one-of-a-kind geological characteristics, such as its high peaks, alpine tundra, and waterfalls, it is a favorite destination for hikers, climbers, and others who are interested in nature.

Acadia National Park

Acadia National Park is one of the national parks in the United States that receives the most visitors each year. The park is situated on the coast of Maine. The park extends over a total area of more than 47,000 acres and includes not just Mount Desert Island but also a number of additional, smaller islands. It is a haven for many different species of wildlife as well as forests and coastlines. At Acadia National Park, visitors can enjoy a wide variety of activities, including scenic drives, hiking paths, and activities on the lake.

Acadia National Park, which may be found on the rocky coast of Maine, is home to a number of different kinds of interesting geological formations. The highest point in the park is Cadillac Mountain, which rises to a height of 1,530 feet above sea level and is known for being the first location in the United States to witness the sunrise. In addition to those two mountains, the park contains a number of other mountains, such as Sargent Mountain and Penobscot Mountain.

The coastline of Acadia National Park is another one of the park's most popular features, due to its rugged cliffs, rocky beaches, and breathtaking vistas of the Atlantic Ocean. The park is home to a number of attractive lighthouses, the most notable of which are the Egg Rock Lighthouse and the Bass Harbor Head Lighthouse.

There are many different kinds of animals that call Acadia National Park their home, such as moose, black bears, white-tailed deer, and bobcats. Within the confines of the park, over 330 different kinds of birds have been identified, making it an important location for people who like birdwatching. It is possible for tourists to catch a glimpse of ospreys, peregrine falcons, and bald eagles swooping above the beach.

Hiking, camping, cycling, kayaking, and rock climbing are just few of the many different types of outdoor activities that may be enjoyed at Acadia National Park. The park contains more than 120 miles of hiking paths, which range in difficulty from casual strolls to rigorous climbs up steep slopes. The Jordan Pond Path, the Precipice Trail, and the Beehive Trail are three of the most well-known and often visited hiking paths in the area.

Cycling is another well-liked activity that can be enjoyed in the park, which features more than 75 kilometers (nearly 45 miles) of carriage roads. In the early 1900s, John D. Rockefeller Jr. constructed the carriage routes, which now provide breathtaking vistas of the park's forests and shoreline.

There are a number of organizations in Acadia National Park that provide guided kayak excursions of the park's coastline and islands. Kayaking is another one of the park's most popular activities. Visitors get the opportunity to witness marine life while paddling through protected bays and exploring the park's numerous islands.

There are various visitor centers and museums located within Acadia National Park that provide information about the park's history, as well as its geology and wildlife. The Hulls Cove Visitor Center is the primary visitor center for the park. It features displays on the natural history and cultural history of the area, in addition to providing information about hiking and camping. In addition, the Sieur de Monts Nature Center and the Islesford Historical Museum both provide visitors with exhibits and information regarding the natural and cultural history of the area.

It is imperative that visitors to Acadia National Park observe all of the rules and regulations that pertain to proper conduct while in the park. Visitors are expected to show respect for the local species, refrain from approaching or feeding the animals, and bring appropriate clothing and gear for the park's secluded position and high temperatures. It is also essential to put the Leave No Trace principles into reality, which include removing all waste from the area and avoiding hurting the surrounding plants or rock formations.

In addition, guests should be aware of the specific rules and restrictions that apply to the national park, such as the ban on the use of personal watercraft and the need to obtain a permission in order to go rock climbing. Additionally, campfires and the use of drones are not permitted within the park; therefore, before making travel arrangements, it is imperative that you check the park's website or any visitor centers for the most up-to-date laws.

In conclusion, Acadia National Park is an incredible location that has much to offer visitors of all ages and interests. Acadia National Park is a place that all people who have a passion for the great outdoors should go at least once because of its breathtaking coastline, singular geological formations, and abundant opportunities for outdoor recreation, as well as its various visitor centers.

Great Smoky Mountains National Park

One of the national parks in the United States with the highest number of visitors is the Great Smoky Mountains National Park, which is situated on the state line between North Carolina and Tennessee. The park is one of the largest protected areas in the eastern United States, comprising approximately 500,000 acres of land, making it one of the largest parks in the region. At Great Smoky Mountains National Park, visitors can enjoy a wide variety of activities, including scenic drives, hiking trails, and opportunities to watch wildlife.

The Great Smoky Mountains National Park gets its name from the haze which often covers the highest summits of the mountains. The

Appalachian Mountain range, which is located in the eastern United States, can be found in this park in its natural habitat. Clingmans Dome, which stands at an elevation of 6,643 feet above mean sea level, is the highest point in the park.

The park is home to a number of interesting geological phenomena, such as waterfalls, caverns, and rock formations. Chimney Tops, which give breathtaking views of the park from their summit, and the Roaring Fork Motor Nature Trail, which travels through the park's gorgeous valleys and woodlands, are two of the most popular features in the park. Both of these trails are open to motorized vehicles.

There are many different kinds of animals that call Great Smoky Mountains National Park their home, such as black bears, white-tailed deer, elk, and coyotes. Within the confines of the park, over 200 different kinds of birds have been identified, making it an important location for people who like birdwatching. The park is home to a resident population of peregrine falcons, which can be seen by guests along with songbirds, raptors, and ducks.

The Great Smoky Mountains National Park is home to a diverse selection of outdoor pursuits, such as hiking, camping, fishing, and watching animals. The park contains more than 800 miles of hiking paths, which range in difficulty from casual strolls to rigorous climbs up steep slopes. The Appalachian Trail, the Alum Cave Trail, and the Rainbow Falls Trail are three of the most well-known and well-visited hiking paths in the United States.

Tent and recreational vehicle camping are both allowed at the park's many campgrounds, which contribute to the popularity of this pastime within the area. Those who would rather go hiking and camping in more remote places may appreciate the park's selection of various backcountry campsites.

Fishing is another sport that is very well-liked in Great Smoky Mountains National Park. The park contains a number of streams and rivers, making it an ideal setting for fishers. It is possible for visitors to catch trout, bass, and other fish species when fishing in the park; however, they are required to have a fishing license that is still active and to comply with park restrictions regulating fishing places and catch limits.

Great Smoky Mountains National Park is home to a number of visitor centers and museums that are devoted to preserving and showcasing the natural and cultural heritage of the surrounding area. The Sugarlands Visitor Center is the primary visitor center for the park and features exhibits on the natural and cultural history of the region. Additionally, the center provides information on hiking trails and camping areas. In addition, the Mountain Farm Museum and the Oconaluftee Visitor Center both provide exhibits and information regarding the history and culture of the park.

It is imperative that visitors to Great Smoky Mountains National Park observe all of the rules and regulations that pertain to proper conduct while inside the park. Visitors are expected to show respect for the local species, refrain from approaching or feeding the animals, and bring appropriate clothing and gear for the park's secluded position and high temperatures. It is also essential to put the Leave No Trace principles into practice, which include removing all waste from the area and avoiding hurting the surrounding plants or rock formations.

In addition, visitors need to be aware of the specific rules and restrictions that apply to the park, such as the ban on the use of off-road vehicles and the need to obtain a permission in order to camp in the backcountry. Additionally, campfires and the use of drones are not permitted within the park; therefore, before making travel arrangements, it is necessary that you check the park's website or any visitor centers for the most up-to-date laws.

To summarize, Great Smoky Mountains National Park is an amazing place to visit because it caters to visitors of all ages and interests. Great Smoky Mountains National Park is a site that everybody who enjoys spending time in nature should make an effort to see at least once. This park is known for its breathtaking waterfalls and mountain peaks, as well as its abundance of outdoor activities and visitor centers.

Glacier National Park

Glacier National Park, which can be found in the upper right-hand corner of Montana, is often regarded as one of the most beautiful natural areas in all of the United States. The national park is well-known for the towering mountain peaks, glistening lakes, and varied animal species that can be found there. The fact that Glacier National Park contains one of the largest unspoiled ecosystems in the continental United States contributes to the park's popularity as a destination for people who enjoy being outside and appreciating nature.

The majority of Glacier National Park is made up of mountainous terrain and the park as a whole covers more than one million acres. The Middle Fork of the Flathead River runs through the park and divides the Lewis Range and the Livingston Range, both of which are mountain ranges that may be found inside the park. Over 130 named lakes can be found within the park, including Lake McDonald and Saint Mary Lake, both of which provide visitors with breathtaking perspectives and opportunity to participate in water-based activities.

The unique history of the region has left its mark on the geology of Glacier National Park. Over sixty glaciers, many of which date back to the most recent ice age, may be found inside the park. Throughout the park, these glaciers are responsible for the formation of magnificent peaks and ridges, as well as the carving out of valleys. The park is also home to a number of important geological structures, one of which is known as the Garden Wall and is characterized by a vertical cliff face that is a favorite spot for climbers and hikers.

Glacier National Park is home to a wide variety of animals, such as grizzly bears, black bears, mountain goats, and elk, among other species. Over 260 different kinds of birds have been identified within the confines of the park, making it an important location for anyone who are interested in birdwatching. In addition to trumpeter swans, visitors might catch a glimpse of bald eagles, peregrine falcons, and other species of raptors that call this area home.

Hiking, camping, fishing, and even just looking at wild animals are just some of the outdoor pursuits that may be enjoyed in Glacier National Park. There are approximately 700 miles of hiking paths throughout the park, ranging from easy strolls to challenging hikes up steep slopes. Some of the trails are even wheelchair accessible. The Highline Trail, the Grinnell Glacier Trail, and the Iceberg Lake

Trail are three of the most well-known and well-used hiking paths in the area.

Tent and recreational vehicle camping are both allowed at the park's many campgrounds, which contribute to the popularity of this pastime within the area. Those who would rather go hiking and camping in more remote places may appreciate the park's selection of various backcountry campsites.

Due to the presence of a number of lakes and streams within the park's boundaries, fishing is another one of Glacier National Park's most well-liked activities. It is possible for visitors to catch trout, bass, and other fish species when fishing in the park; however, they are required to have a fishing license that is still active and to comply with park restrictions regulating fishing places and catch limits.

There are a number of visitor centers and museums located within Glacier National area. These centers and museums provide information about the history, geology, and wildlife of the area. The Apgar Visitor Center is the primary tourist center for the park and features exhibits on the natural and cultural history of the region. Additionally, the center provides information on hiking trails and camping areas. The Logan Pass Visitor Center is another popular location in the park since it provides visitors with access to the Highline Trail as well as breathtaking views of the park's mountain peaks.

It is imperative that visitors to Glacier National Park observe all of the rules and regulations that pertain to proper conduct within the park. Visitors are expected to show respect for the local species, refrain from approaching or feeding the animals, and bring appropriate clothing and gear for the park's secluded position and high temperatures. It is also essential to put the Leave No Trace principles into reality, which include removing all waste from the area and avoiding hurting the surrounding plants or rock formations.

In addition, visitors need to be aware of the specific rules and restrictions that apply to the park, such as the ban on the use of off-road vehicles and the need to obtain a permission in order to camp in the backcountry. Additionally, campfires and the use of drones are not permitted within the park; therefore, before making travel arrangements, it is necessary that you check the park's website or any visitor centers for the most current laws.

In conclusion, Glacier National Park is a stunning location that has something to offer visitors of all ages and interests. This wonderful national park offers visitors a wealth of opportunity to discover and appreciate its many wonders, from the park's breathtaking landscapes to the wide variety of outdoor pursuits and species it contains. Glacier National Park is a place that should not be missed, regardless of whether you consider yourself an avid hiker, a nature enthusiast, or just someone who is searching for a calm escape.

Joshua Tree National Park

Joshua Tree National Park, which can be found in the southeast corner of the state of California, is a one-of-a-kind desert attraction that is visited by people from all over the world. The park is well-known for its incredible rock formations, the flora and animals of the desert, and the famous Joshua Trees that are scattered across the terrain. Visitors to Joshua Tree National Park are afforded the opportunity to venture out into the desert wilderness, discover the region's distinctive geology and animals, and participate in a wide range of outdoor activities.

The Mojave Desert and the Colorado Desert are two separate desert ecosystems that meet in Joshua Tree National Park, which is located at the junction of these two deserts. The park encompasses an area of more than 790,000 acres and is distinguished by the extraordinary rock formations, towering monoliths, and broad desert vistas that can be found there. The geology of the park was formed over the course of millions of years by tectonic action and erosion, both of which contributed to the development of the park's breathtaking environment, which visitors can now enjoy.

Joshua Tree National Park is home to a diverse collection of plant and animal species, in spite of the severe conditions of the surrounding desert. Visitors have a good chance of spotting a wide range of animals during their time in the area, such as bighorn sheep, coyotes, jackrabbits, and a number of different species of birds. In addition, the park is home to a number of different kinds of reptiles and amphibians, the most famous of which is the desert tortoise.

Hiking, rock climbing, camping, and stargazing are just some of the outdoor activities that tourists can enjoy during their time at Joshua Tree National Park in California. The expansive network of hiking trails in the park offers something for hikers of all ability levels, with possibilities ranging from casual nature walks to challenging backcountry hikes. The park is a great place to get outside and enjoy the great outdoors. The Lost Palms Oasis Trail, the Ryan Mountain Trail, and the Barker Dam Trail are three of the most well-known hiking routes in this area.

Rock climbing is another activity that attracts a large number of visitors to Joshua Tree National Park. The park has more than 8,000 recognized climbing routes spread out across the landscape. The distinctive granite formations of the park provide climbers with a wide range of climbing opportunities, from straightforward boulder issues to difficult multi-pitch routes.

Tent and recreational vehicle camping are both allowed at the park's many campgrounds, which contribute to the popularity of this recreation within the area. Those who would rather go hiking and camping in more remote places may appreciate the park's selection of various backcountry campsites.

Stargazing is consistently cited as one of the most well-liked things to do in Joshua Tree National Park. There are some of the best opportunities for stargazing in the United States to be had in this park due to its distant position and the clear desert skies. As a result of the park's year-round stargazing events and ranger-led astronomy discussions, it has become a popular destination for amateur astronomers.

There are a number of visitor centers and museums located within Joshua Tree National Park. These centers and museums provide information about the history, geology, and animals of the park. The Joshua Tree Visitor Center is the primary visitor center for the park. It features exhibits on the natural and cultural history of the region, in addition to providing information about hiking and camping. The Oasis Visitor Center is another popular attraction in the park. It provides information on the desert habitat and the animals that live in the desert.

It is imperative that visitors to Joshua Tree National Park observe all of the park's rules and regulations pertaining to proper conduct while in the park. Visitors are expected to show respect for the local species, refrain from approaching or feeding the animals, and bring appropriate clothing and gear for the park's secluded position and high temperatures. It is also essential to put the Leave No Trace principles into reality, which include removing all waste from the area and avoiding hurting the surrounding plants or rock formations.

In addition, visitors need to be aware of the specific rules and regulations that apply to the park, such as the ban on off-road vehicles and drones, as well as the necessity of obtaining a permission in order to camp in the backcountry. Campfires are prohibited within the park; thus, before making travel arrangements, it is essential to check the park's website or visit one of its visitor centers to obtain the most recent regulations.

In general, Joshua Tree National Park provides a breathtaking and one-of-a-kind scenery that is ideal for people who enjoy being outside, who are fans of nature, and who are looking to find inspiration and revitalize their creative spirit. Anyone who is going to be in Southern California should absolutely make a point of going to this place. Not only does it have a large and harsh environment, but it also has a rich history and is culturally significant.

Arches National Park

Arches National Park, which can be found in the eastern part of Utah, is a must-see location due to the amazing geological formations and natural arches that can be found there. The park encompasses approximately 76,000 acres and features over 2,000 natural stone arches, in addition to towering sandstone formations, steep canyons, and winding hiking paths.

Since it was built in 1929, the park has developed into a well-known attraction for people who enjoy being outdoors, who are interested in nature, and who are photographers. Visitors have the opportunity to learn about the geology and history of the region here, as well as experience the distinctive terrain.

Arches National Park has a fascinating and intricate geological past that is well worth exploring. The park can be found on the Colorado Plateau, an area that was formerly submerged under a warm, shallow sea. Layers of sandstone, shale, and several other types of sedimentary rock were deposited in this region as a result of uplift and erosion that occurred over a period of millions of years.

After being exposed to the elements for a period of time, the rock layers began to erode and eventually formed distinctive geological structures such as fins, spires, and arches. The arches that can be seen throughout the park are the result of a combination of weathering and erosion, with elements such as wind, water, and ice chipping away at the softer sandstone layers.

Arches National Park contains arches that range in length from just a few feet to more than 300 feet in length. The most well-known arch in the park is called Delicate Arch, and it is a freestanding arch that has evolved into an iconic representation of the park.

Hiking, rock climbing, and camping are just some of the activities that are available for guests to enjoy during their time in Arches National Park. The park has more than 18 miles of paved roads and more than 50 miles of hiking trails, which range from short strolls to long, demanding excursions. Easy walks are also available.

The Devil's Garden Trail is one of the most well-known hiking routes in the park. It takes hikers to a number of magnificent arches, including Landscape Arch, the longest arch in North America. Along with being an excellent way to get to know the park, the route provides some breathtaking vistas of the area's natural scenery.

Those who are interested in rock climbing will find that Arches National Park provides a wide selection of climbing routes that are suitable for climbers of all skill levels. Climbers can put their talents to the test on the towering sandstone formations in the park while also enjoying the one-of-a-kind experience that comes with climbing there.

Arches National Park has two different campgrounds for people to stay in while they are there, as camping is another popular pastime in the park. There are 50 campsites available at the Devils Garden Campground, but the Willow Flat Campground, which is far smaller, only has 12. Both of the campgrounds provide visitors with breathtaking vistas of the area's topography and serve as an excellent option for spending the night inside the park.

Although Arches National Park is most famous for the geological structures that may be found there, it is also home to a wide diversity of animal species. Animals such as desert bighorn sheep, coyotes, foxes, and a wide diversity of bird species can be seen by visitors to the park.

The desert tortoise is a species of reptile that is slow-moving and has adapted to survive in the harsh environment of the desert. It is one of the most interesting and distinctive animals that can be found in the park. Visitors are asked to keep their distance from the park's native animals out of respect for them and to ensure their own safety.

Arches National Park charges an entrance fee and is open throughout the entire year for visitors to enjoy. Although the park is most popular during the warmer summer months when temperatures are most agreeable, it is open throughout the year and may be visited in the spring and fall as well.

Visitors are strongly recommended to bring lots of water, sunscreen, and other protective gear, as well as clothing and footwear suitable for hiking and other types of outdoor activities. In addition, the park provides visitors with a selection of educational programs and ranger-led tours, so that they can get additional knowledge on the geology, history, and wildlife of the region.

Arches National Park, with its one-of-a-kind and breathtaking scenery, is an excellent destination for anyone who enjoy the great outdoors, who adore nature, and who are interested in photography. Because of its unique geological structures, natural arches, and abundant wildlife, it is an absolutely essential site.

A few more renowned national parks for RV camping

When it comes to camping in an RV, the United States is home to a large number of national parks, each of which provides visitors with a wealth of exciting chances for outdoor adventure and discovery. There are a number of other well-known national parks that are suitable for RV camping, in addition to the places that have already been mentioned.

Bryce Canyon National Park, which can be found in the southwestern corner of Utah, is famous for the unusual geological structures that can be seen there, such as tall hoodoos and natural amphitheaters. There are a number of campgrounds within the park that are suitable for RV camping, including the North and Sunset campgrounds. Both of these campgrounds include sites equipped with electricity hookups. In addition, the park features scenic drives, hiking trails, and opportunities to view the night sky.

Shenandoah National Park is a well-known site for RV camping due to its location in the Blue Ridge Mountains in the state of Virginia. The park is home to a number of campgrounds, one of which being the Big Meadows Campground, which provides electrical hookups for recreational vehicles. In addition to this, the park features scenic roads, hiking paths, and opportunities to view wildlife and birds.

Grand Teton National Park, which may be found in the far northwestern part of Wyoming, is a popular location for RV camping. There are a number of campgrounds within the park, including Colter Bay Village and Signal Mountain Campground, both of which include RV parking spots that are wired for electricity. The park also provides chances for activities such as hiking, fishing, observing wildlife, and driving through scenic areas.

RV campers will find Olympic National Park, which is located in the state of Washington, to be an attractive and varied destination. The park features a number of campgrounds, two of which are the Sol Duc Hot Springs Resort Campground and the Kalaloch Campground. Both of these campgrounds provide RV sites equipped with electrical hookups. The park also provides chances for activities including as hiking, beachcombing, observing local wildlife, and experiencing the Hoh Rainforest.

Death Valley National Park is famous for both its scorching temperatures and its otherworldly scenery, and it is located on the border of California and Nevada. The park features a number of RV-friendly campgrounds, including the Furnace Creek Campground, which is equipped with full connections for recreational vehicles. Visitors have the opportunity to participate in activities such as stargazing, beautiful drives, and hiking paths.

Petrified Forest National Park is well-known for its old petrified wood and vibrant badlands, both of which may be found in the northeastern part of Arizona. There is one campground in the park that is suitable for RV camping, and all of the sites come equipped with electrical hookups. Visitors are able to take pleasure in scenic roads, hiking trails, and opportunities to view wildlife and birds throughout their time here.

The breathtaking beauty of the badlands and the wide variety of animals that call Theodore Roosevelt National Park in North Dakota home are two of the park's most famous features. Visitors have the opportunity to explore the park's harsh terrain while remaining in the luxury of their own RVs due to the presence of multiple campgrounds that offer RV spots. Hiking, observing animals, and touring the park's historic landmarks are among the most well-liked things to do at Theodore Roosevelt National Park.

Some of the park's most well-known historical sites are Roosevelt's Maltese Cross Cabin and the Painted Canyon Visitor Center.

Overall, RV camping gives tourists the chance to see some of the most breathtaking national parks in the United States while still being able to take advantage of the conveniences that come with their own recreational vehicles. There is bound to be a national park that accommodates recreational vehicles, given the variety of parks that provide such facilities.

Chapter III

Exploring America's Most Beautiful Landscapes on Wheels

Trails for biking and hiking in national parks

Visitors get the opportunity to explore spectacular landscapes and get up close and personal with amazing species when they go to national parks, which are among the most beautiful and distinctive places in the world. And getting out on foot or on a bike and exploring the park's trails is one of the finest ways to take advantage of everything these parks have to offer.

It is not difficult to comprehend why hiking is one of the most well-liked outdoor activities available in national parks. Hikers of all skill levels are able to select a trail that matches their abilities and interests because of the availability of countless paths spanning hundreds of kilometres. Just a few of the national parks' hiking routes that are considered to be among the best are as follows:

One of the most famous trails in Grand Canyon National Park, the Bright Angel Trail is known for providing hikers with breathtaking vistas of the Grand Canyon. The trail lowers approximately 4,500 feet to the Colorado River as it winds through the red granite formations. The trail has a round-trip distance of 12 miles, and hikers should be prepared to spend an entire day exploring the trail and soaking in the stunning scenery along the way.

The Mist Trail is a well-known trail that can be found in Yosemite National Park. It leads hikers to the top of Vernal Fall and provides them with breathtaking views of the waterfall and the valley in which it is located. Hikers should come prepared for a difficult ascent because the terrain is not only steep but also has the potential to be slippery. The round-trip distance of the trail is just 2.4 miles.

Great Smoky Mountains National Park is home to a section of the world-famous Appalachian Trail, which runs for more than 71 miles through the park and provides hikers with the opportunity to experience the stunning landscape of the Appalachian Mountains. The track is well-marked and kept in good condition, making it an excellent choice that is suitable for hikers of all experience levels.

The Angels Landing Trail is a strenuous trail located in Zion National Park that climbs approximately 1,500 feet to the summit of Angels Landing. Hikers that take this trail are rewarded with breathtaking vistas of Zion Canyon along the way. The track is only 5 miles round-trip, but it is quite steep and requires hikers to navigate tiny trails that have tremendous drop-offs on either side.

The Highline Trail in Glacier National Park is a breathtaking trail that is over 11 miles long and runs through the center of the park. It provides hikers with breathtaking views of the mountains and valleys that are located in the surrounding area. The track is clearly defined and not overly difficult to follow, making it an excellent option for hikers of varying levels of experience.

Biking is another popular way to tour national parks, since it allows visitors to cover more land than they would be able to on foot while allowing them to continue to appreciate the stunning natural scenery all around them. The following is a list of some of the most notable bicycle routes in national parks:

The Going-to-the-Sun Road in Glacier National Park is an iconic road that offers bikers amazing views of the park. The road winds through the mountains and provides stunning panoramas of snow-capped peaks and pristine lakes. Bikers can experience the Going-to-the-Sun Road. The road is approximately 50 miles long and can be traveled in a single day; however, cyclists should be prepared for some difficult ascents and descents along the route.

The Cades Cove Loop Road in Great Smoky Mountains National Park is an 11-mile loop that provides cyclists with the opportunity to experience some of the most picturesque portions of the park, including historic homesteads and spectacular vistas of the surrounding mountains. The road is part of the park's Cades Cove area. Because of the road's lack of significant elevation change and the simplicity of its layout, it is an excellent choice for cyclists of varying degrees of experience.

The White Rim Trail in Canyonlands National Park is an excellent option for seasoned mountain cyclists who are searching for a course that will test their skills. The path is more than 100 miles long and winds through the park, providing hikers with breathtaking vistas of the canyons and rock formations in the area. Because riders are required to camp overnight at predetermined locations along the trail, they should be prepared to spend multiple days out on the trail.

The Munds Wagon Trail is a route that is located in Red Rock State Park and is 7.5 miles long. It winds through a variety of landscapes and terrain and provides hikers and cyclists with breathtaking views of the surrounding red rock formations. Because the track is not very difficult and there are just a few modest inclines, it is an excellent choice for cyclists who are at an intermediate skill level.

Last but not least, the Flume track in Lake Tahoe is an absolutely gorgeous track that provides bikers with breathtaking views of the lake and the mountains that surround it. Because of its short length (just over 14 miles) and moderate difficulty, the trail is an excellent choice for cyclists of varying levels of experience.

When touring national parks by foot or by bike, there are a few crucial things to keep in mind, regardless of whether you are an experienced hiker or biker or whether you are just starting out. These guidelines are as follows:

The first and most important step is to make a detailed plan. It is important to do some study about the path or route that you intend to take before setting out on a hike or a bike trip. Find out the distance, the type of terrain, and the amount of difficulty, and make sure to bring a lot of water and snacks with you. This will assist to guarantee that you are well prepared for the adventure that lies ahead and that you are able to take in the breathtaking scenery of the park without being disrupted by any unanticipated challenges.

It is essential that you wear clothing that is suitable for both the climate and the activity in which you will be engaging. Make sure that the clothing you wear is comfortable, appropriate for the weather, and that your shoes are solid and supportive. If you ride a bike, you should always wear a helmet and think about purchasing other safety gear like knee and elbow protectors.

It is imperative that visitors adhere to the Leave No Trace rules when they are in national parks. Protecting our nation's national parks, which include some of the world's most precious and unique ecosystems, should be a priority for everyone. Be careful to carry out all of your rubbish and dispose of it in the appropriate manner. Additionally, try to avoid upsetting the native plants and animals. This involves keeping to the pathways that have been established, avoiding trampling vegetation, and having as little of an influence as possible on the surrounding area.

In addition, it is essential to show proper respect for the animals that make national parks their home. There is a diverse array of animals that call national parks their home, and it is essential to show them the proper amount of room and refrain from getting too close to them. Maintain a safe distance, do not attempt to feed or touch wild animals, and always keep your distance from them. This not only keeps you safe, but also ensures that the animals may continue to behave and live in their natural environments without interference.

Finally, it is essential to adhere to the laws and regulations of the park. It is imperative that visitors adhere to the specific rules and regulations of each national park, as doing so will both aid in the preservation of the park's natural ecosystem and guarantee that everyone will have a pleasant and secure time there. This may include things like staying on trails that have been designated for that purpose, not camping in locations that have not been designated for that purpose, and obeying park closures and other limitations.

In conclusion, hiking and bicycling are two of the best ways to experience the breathtaking natural beauty that can be found in national parks all around the United States. There are trails and routes available in national parks that are suited to people of all skill levels and interests, from the challenging ascents of the Bright Angel Trail in Grand Canyon National Park to the breathtaking panoramas of the Going-to-the-Sun Road in Glacier National Park. Visitors may enjoy everything that these wonderful parks have to offer while also helping to safeguard and preserve these natural riches for future generations by adhering to some key suggestions and standards throughout their time in the parks.

Scenic drives and viewpoints

Many people believe that hitting the open road and embarking on a scenic drive is the best way to take in the breathtaking landscapes of a particular area. The United States is home to innumerable scenic drives and overlooks that provide amazing perspectives of some of the country's most stunning landscapes. These drives and viewpoints may be found anywhere from winding mountain roads to coastal motorways.

Scenic drives are a popular means by which to discover the natural beauty of a place. They give tourists the opportunity to take in breathtaking panoramas and scenery while remaining in the convenience of their own vehicles. The following is a list of just some of the most beautiful drives in the United States:

The Pacific Coast Highway in California is a famous highway that runs for more than 650 miles down the coast of California. Travelers who take this route are treated to breathtaking panoramas of the Pacific Ocean and the rough coastline. The trip is especially breathtaking in the spring, when wildflowers are in bloom, and in the fall, when the leaves on the trees all around turn a golden color.

The Blue Ridge Parkway is a 469-mile scenic road that runs through the picturesque Blue Ridge Mountains, affording travelers breathtaking views of the surrounding valleys and peaks. The Blue Ridge Parkway is located in the states of Virginia and North Carolina. When autumn arrives and the leaves on the trees change into a kaleidoscope of colors, the trip takes on an especially breathtaking quality.

The Going-to-the-Sun Road is a beautiful road that is located in the state of Montana. It is fifty miles long and winds through the middle of Glacier National Park, providing visitors with breathtaking views of the surrounding mountains and valleys. The trip is absolutely breathtaking at any time of year, but it is especially breathtaking in the summer when the wildflowers are in bloom and the mountains still have snow on their peaks.

The Million Dollar Highway is a route that is located in the state of Colorado. It is a section of highway that is 25 miles long and runs through the San Juan Mountains. This highway offers breathtaking views of the surrounding mountains and valleys. When autumn arrives and the leaves on the aspen trees that are all around you turn a golden color, the drive is especially beautiful.

The Great River Road is a picturesque route that spans 3,000 miles and follows the Mississippi River from its source in Minnesota all the way to its end in Louisiana. The journey takes travelers to a total of ten states, during which they will have the opportunity to learn about the region's rich cultural and natural heritage.

Another well-liked option to soak in the natural splendor of an area is to visit its various viewpoints, which provide tourists the opportunity to get a better look at the region's breathtaking panoramas and landscapes. The following is a list of some of the most spectacular viewpoints in the United States:

The Grand Canyon, located in Grand Canyon National Park in Arizona, is often regarded as one of the most recognizable natural sights in the United States. Visitors to the Grand Canyon are treated to breathtaking panoramas of the rock formations and other canyons in the area. Mather Point, Yavapai Point, and Lipan Point are considered to be some of the most breathtaking vantage spots in the park.

Geysers, waterfalls, and hot springs are just some of the natural marvels that can be found in Yellowstone National Park, which is located in the state of Wyoming. The park is known for the breathtaking views it provides of the countryside in the area. Artist Point, Grand View, and Hayden Valley are regarded as some of the most breathtaking vantage spots in the park.

Acadia National Park in Maine is home to some of the most breathtaking coastal views in the United States. The park gives tourists the opportunity to experience rocky shoreline and waves that are pounding against the shore. The vantage points atop Cadillac Mountain, at Jordan Pond, and on Otter Cliff are among the most breathtaking in the park.

Rocky Mountain National Park in Colorado is home to some of the most breathtaking mountain scenery in the United States, giving visitors the opportunity to see snow-capped peaks and alpine meadows. The park is located in the state of Colorado. Trail Ridge Road, Bear Lake Overlook, and Moraine Park are known to have some of the most breathtaking vantage points in the park.

Zion National Park in Utah is home to some of the most breathtaking rock formations and slot canyons in the United States. The park provides visitors with the opportunity to get up close and personal with the distinctive geological features of the local area. Angels Landing, Observation Point, and the Canyon Overlook Trail are three of the trails that lead to some of the best viewpoints in the park.

Whether you're going for a drive through a picturesque area or stopping at a viewpoint, there are a few things you should always keep in mind to make sure you have a pleasant and risk-free time:

It is essential to make preparations in advance before going on a drive with beautiful scenery or going to a viewpoint. Do some research on the region, and be familiar with the distance, the topography, and the level of difficulty. Be sure to pack a lot of water and snacks, and arrange for stops along the journey so that you can get some rest. This will help guarantee that the experience is both safe and pleasurable.

There are many beautiful drives and overlooks that are located within national parks or other protected areas, and it is essential to adhere to the rules and regulations in order to assist in the preservation of the natural environment and guarantee that all visitors have an experience that is both safe and pleasurable. This involves staying on trails and lookout spots that have been designated for use, packing out all rubbish, and disposing of it in the appropriate manner.

It is imperative that visitors to a popular viewpoint or beautiful drive keep in mind that there may be other people in the area. It is important to be mindful of the experiences that other visitors are having and to avoid impeding access to vistas or paths. Additionally, it is essential to wear clothing that is suitable for the climate and terrain, as well as to be ready for shifts in both the temperature and the wind direction.

Lastly, it is essential to practice caution when traveling along picturesque highways and visiting vistas. Keep in mind to obey all of the traffic restrictions and use caution when driving on twisting or tight roads while enjoying the beautiful scenery. When going to a viewpoint, be sure to stay on the routes and viewing spots that have been designated for visitors and keep a safe distance from the edge of any cliffs or other potential dangers.

In conclusion, scenic drives and overlooks provide tourists with the opportunity to experience the natural beauty of the United States in a way that is both distinctive and unforgettable. These opportunities can range from the breathtaking coastline views offered by the Pacific Coast Highway to the rough mountain panoramas presented by Rocky Mountain National Park. Visitors may enjoy everything that these wonderful locations have to offer while also helping to safeguard and preserve these natural treasures for future generations by adhering to a few key suggestions and principles that are vital to keep in mind.

Wildlife watching and birding

Visitors are provided with an unique and exhilarating opportunity to develop a profoundly meaningful connection with the natural world when they are able to observe animals and birds in the environments in which they are native. The United States is home to an astounding variety of animal and bird species, making it a great destination for people who are interested in wildlife viewing and birding. From towering moose in the forests of Alaska to brilliant hummingbirds in the deserts of Arizona, the United States is home to an incredible assortment of wildlife and bird species.

Watching wild animals in their natural settings is a favorite pastime of people who are interested in nature since it gives tourists the opportunity to see some of the most well-known and unique animals in the country. The following places in the United States are some of those considered to be among the best for wildlife viewing:

Yellowstone National Park, which is located in Wyoming, is famous for the vast diversity of animals that can be seen there. Some of these animals include grizzly bears, wolves, bison, and elk. Lamar Valley, Hayden Valley, and the shores of Yellowstone Lake are among the most excellent locations in the park for seeing the park's diverse animal population. Visitors have the option of participating in guided tours or venturing out on their own to get a better look at these wonderful animals.

There are many rare and endangered animals that call Everglades National Park in Florida their home. Some of these animals include American crocodiles, manatees, and the elusive Florida panther. Visitors have the option of participating in guided tours or venturing out on their own to get a closer look at these wonderful animals.

Denali National Park in Alaska is another well-known location for seeing wild animals in their natural habitat. The park is home to a broad range of species that is representative of Alaska, such as grizzly bears, moose, and caribou. Visitors have the option of participating in guided tours or venturing out on their own to get a better look at these wonderful animals.

The Great Smoky Mountains National Park spans both Tennessee and North Carolina, and is famous for the breathtaking scenery and abundant species that can be found there. The park is home to a wide variety of animal species, including black bears, white-tailed deer, and elk, among others. Visitors have the option of exploring the park on their own or participating in guided tours in order to view these amazing creatures in their natural environments.

Finally, Grand Teton National Park in the state of Wyoming is home to a vast array of animal species, some of which include grizzly bears, wolves, and bison. Visitors have the option of participating in guided tours or venturing out on their own to get a better look at these wonderful animals.

Birdwatching is another well-liked pastime among nature lovers since it gives tourists the opportunity to witness some of the country's most stunning and distinctive bird species in the environments in which they evolved naturally. The following places in the United States are among the top spots in the country for birdwatching:

Cape May, New Jersey, is widely regarded as one of the East Coast's premier locations for bird watching. Cape May, which is situated at the extreme southwestern end of the state of New Jersey, is an ideal place for birdwatchers to visit in order to observe the annual migration of thousands of birds. Visitors have the opportunity to view a large number of species, such as warblers, hawks, and waterfowl, during the migrations that occur in the spring and fall. Cape May Point State Park and the Higbee Beach

Wildlife Management Area are two of the places that are considered to be among the best in the region for birding.

The Bosque del Apache National Wildlife Refuge in New Mexico is widely regarded as the best location for birdwatchers to visit in the southwestern region of the United States. The wildlife refuge is home to a wide variety of bird species, some of which include bald eagles, sandhill cranes, and snow geese. Visitors have the option of participating in guided tours or venturing out on their own to get a better look at these beautiful birds.

For those interested in birdwatching, the Point Reyes National Seashore in California is an absolute must-see location on the West Coast. The park is home to a large number of different bird species, some of which include hawks, pelicans, and ospreys. Visitors have the option of exploring the park on their own or participating in guided tours in order to view these magnificent birds in the environments in which they were naturally found.

The Magee Marsh Wildlife Area in Ohio is widely regarded as one of the best places to go birding in the Midwest. The region is well-known for the remarkable range of migrating bird species that can be seen there. During the spring and fall migrations, tourists have the opportunity to view a vast variety of warblers, thrushes, and flycatchers. The Black Swamp Bird Observatory and the Ottawa National Wildlife Refuge are two of the places in this region that are considered to be among the best for bird watching.

Lastly, Southeast Arizona is widely regarded as one of the premier locations in the United States for bird watching. The area is home to a diverse collection of exotic and endangered bird species, such as the painted redstart, vermilion flycatcher, and the beautiful trogon. Chiricahua Mountains, Ramsey Canyon Preserve, and the Chiricahua National Monument are among the top locations in the region for bird watching.

When venturing out into the natural world, it is crucial to keep the following things in mind, regardless of whether you are an experienced birdwatcher or a beginner wildlife watcher:

To begin, it is absolutely necessary to have respect for animals and the environments in which they live. This entails maintaining a safe distance and avoiding getting too close to the animals in any way, shape, or form. Never attempt to touch or feed wild animals, and always make sure to stay on approved trails and paths to prevent causing harm to the environments in which they live.

When it comes to your outfit, it is essential to wear clothes that are comfortable and suited for the weather, as well as shoes that are supportive and strong. If you want to get a better look at the birds you're observing while birding, you might want to consider purchasing a set of binoculars or a spotting scope. It is possible that you will additionally need to bring certain equipment, such as hiking poles, insect repellent, or sunscreen, depending on the region and the activity. Doing some preliminary research about the location might help you determine what items you should carry with you.

Patience is a virtue that should be practiced when going nature watching or birdwatching. It is crucial to have patience and to take pleasure in the experience of being in nature because it may take some time before you see the species that you are expecting to observe. Learning about the species you are expecting to see can also make your trip more enjoyable. This will enable you to identify them if and when you do come across them, as well as give you a better understanding of the distinctive behaviors and features that are associated with each species.

In conclusion, wildlife watching and birdwatching offer tourists the opportunity to interact with the natural world in a way that is both profound and meaningful. This is true whether they are looking at the towering grizzly bears of Yellowstone National Park or the beautiful hummingbirds of the Sonoran Desert. Visitors may enjoy everything that these wonderful locations have to offer while also helping to safeguard and preserve these natural treasures for future generations by adhering to a few key suggestions and principles that are necessary to keep in mind. There has never been a better moment to enjoy the beautiful scenery that the United States has to offer, regardless of whether you are an experienced wildlife observer or a beginner birdwatcher.

Water activities: kayaking, fishing, and more

Visitors get an unique and thrilling opportunity to connect with the natural environment when they participate in water sports such as kayaking, fishing, and other similar pursuits. The United States of America is home to an astounding variety of waterways, each of which provides an abundance of options for excitement and relaxation. These waterways range from the calm waters of a mountain lake to the raging rapids of a wild river.

Kayaking is a well-liked activity for people who are interested in the natural world since it gives tourists the opportunity to discover the scenic splendor of an area from the vantage point of the water. The following is a list of some of the most popular places to go kayaking in the United States:

Glacier Bay National Park in Alaska is widely regarded as one of the best places in the world to go kayaking. Kayaking is one of the greatest ways to enjoy the natural beauty of the region up close and personal, and this park is home to some of the most breathtaking glaciers and an abundance of animals. Visitors have the option of going on guided tours of the park or paddling around on their own to take in the breathtaking vistas and diverse animals.

Lake Tahoe, which is situated on the state line between California and Nevada, is yet another well-known location for kayaking. Visitors have the opportunity to kayak or canoe through the breathtaking beauty of the mountains that surround the lake and discover secluded coves and beaches due to the lake's exceptionally clean waters.

The Apostle Islands National Lakeshore in the state of Wisconsin is another top site for people who are interested in kayaking. The area is known for its breathtaking sea caves, its untouched beaches, and its plentiful wildlife, all of which combine to make it an ideal location for anyone who enjoy kayaking. Visitors have the option of going on guided tours of the area or paddling around on their own to take in the area's breathtaking landscape and abundant fauna.

Kayaking in Everglades National Park in Florida is a fantastic alternative for nature enthusiasts who want to investigate an ecosystem that is both distinct and rich in biodiversity. The park's twisting rivers offer a one-of-a-kind perspective on the complex environment that the park is home to. This ecosystem is home to a wide range of wildlife, such as American crocodiles and manatees.

Last but not least, the Snake River, which flows through Wyoming and Idaho, is widely recognized as one of the most beautiful rivers in the western United States. Visitors get the opportunity to witness a broad variety of species, including bald eagles and moose, while paddling along the river in a canoe or kayak.

Fishing is another well-liked pastime that can be enjoyed on the water. Anglers can unwind and take in the breathtaking scenery of a location while simultaneously attempting to bring in a prize catch. The following are some of the most popular and productive fishing spots in the United States:

The Kenai River in Alaska is widely regarded as one of the best fishing sites in the world, since it gives tourists the opportunity to reel in salmon, rainbow trout, and other species of fish. Considering visitors of any degree of fishing expertise can go on guided fishing expeditions, this activity is an excellent choice for fishermen of all experience levels, including novices.

The San Juan River in New Mexico is widely recognized as one of the best places to go fly fishing in the United States due to the river's high concentration of trout and its breathtaking natural surroundings. Anglers from all over the United States go to this river to try their luck at fly fishing since the river's water is crystal clear and stays at a constant cool temperature.

Visitors to Lake of the Ozarks in Missouri, which is one of the most popular fishing locations in the Midwest, have the opportunity to reel in a broad range of fish species, including bass, crappie, and catfish. It is possible to go boating and fishing at this lake because of its broad size and the numerous coves and channels that it has.

One of the most popular places to go fly fishing in the United States is the Bighorn River, which can be found flowing through the states of Montana and Wyoming. Anglers can choose to go on guided tours or explore on their own at this destination due to its beautiful surroundings and large number of trout.

Snook, redfish, and tarpon are just some of the saltwater fish that can be found in plenty along the Gulf Coast of Florida, which is home to some of the best fishing in the country. Whether they fish from the shore or a boat, visitors to the Gulf Coast may take advantage of the region's warm waters and stunning beaches while they cast their lines in the hopes of reeling in a monster catch.

In addition to fishing and kayaking, there are an abundance of other water activities that provide visitors the opportunity to interact with the natural world while also having a good time on the water. These activities range from sailing to windsurfing to wakeboarding and more. Just some of them are as follows:

Water sports are a fun and effective opportunity to both take in the breathtaking scenery of a location and work the muscles of the entire body. Stand-up paddleboarding, also known as SUP, is a water sport that has gained popularity over the past few years and is now a well-known hobby. Lake Tahoe, Lake Michigan, and the Florida Keys are all excellent destinations for stand-up paddleboarding lovers.

Snorkeling and scuba diving are two more popular water sports that allow participants to explore the world beneath the surface of the water and get up close and personal with some of the most beautiful marine creatures. Snorkeling and scuba diving are two water sports that are particularly well-known in Hawaii, the Florida Keys, and the Virgin Islands, among other places.

White water rafting is an exhilarating activity that allows participants to navigate their way through rushing rapids while also taking in the breathtaking landscape that the river has to offer. White water rafting is a popular activity, and several rivers, including the Colorado River, the Snake River, and the Ocoee River, are popular destinations.

Finally, water skiing and wakeboarding are two well-liked water sports that give participants the opportunity to glide through the water and engage in exhilarating maneuvers. Some of the most popular locations in the United States for water skiing and wakeboarding are Lake Tahoe, Lake Powell, and the Florida Keys. No matter what type of water sport you participate in, you should always put safety first and take in the breathtaking natural scenery of the area.

Whether you're going kayaking, fishing, or participating in one of the many other activities that can be enjoyed on the water, there are a few essential things to bear in mind to ensure that your time on the water is both safe and enjoyable:

The current state of the weather is undoubtedly one of the most significant aspects to take into account. Because the weather and the water conditions can shift suddenly, it is important to keep an eye on the forecast and be ready for any shifts in the temperature or the direction of the wind. Depending on the nature of the activity you will be participating in, it is essential that you wear the right safety gear such as a life jacket, helmet, or other protection equipment.

In addition, it is extremely important to be aware of your surroundings while you are participating in activities that include water. It is imperative that one does not get too close to potential dangers such as rocks, things that are submerged, or strong currents because of the potential for harm they pose. In addition to being aware of your limits and taking pauses when necessary, you can assist prevent weariness and accidents.

When participating in water sports, one of the most important things to keep in mind is to show the environment proper deference.

It is essential to avoid causing harm to natural habitats and upsetting wildlife wherever possible, whether one is paddling a kayak through a national park or fishing in a nearby river. You can ensure a safe and happy experience by following these safety procedures, which will also allow you to appreciate the natural world's stunning beauty.

In conclusion, water activities provide visitors with the opportunity to connect with the natural world and build experiences that will last a lifetime. These activities can range from kayaking past breathtaking glaciers in Alaska to fishing for prize trout on the San Juan River. Visitors may enjoy everything that these great locations have to offer while also helping to safeguard and preserve these natural riches for future generations by adhering to a few key rules and standards. There has never been a better moment to enjoy the natural beauty of the United States through the delight of water activities, and it doesn't matter if you're an experienced kayaker or a newbie fisherman. There has never been a better time.

Photography tips for capturing the beauty of national parks

Visitors to the United States have the opportunity to connect with nature and enjoy breathtaking landscapes and wildlife up close when they go to one of the country's national parks. National parks are among the most spectacular and awe-inspiring places in the country. For those who are interested in photography, national parks offer a never-ending supply of picture ops that allow them to capture the remarkable variety of the natural surroundings they visit.

When it comes to taking photographs in national parks, making a strategy ahead of time is really necessary. You should do some research on the park that you intend to visit in before so that you can have a sense of the best places for photography, the ideal times of day for lighting, and the types of wildlife or sceneries that you are likely to meet while you are there. Checking the weather forecast and the operating hours of the park are two more things you can do to ensure that you are ready for any potential obstacles or shifts in the environment.

When it comes to taking breathtaking photographs in national parks, having the appropriate equipment can make all the difference in the world. It is possible that you will need to carry certain equipment, such as a tripod, filters, or lenses, in order to take the kind of photography that you are interested in. A durable camera case can assist in protecting your equipment while you are on the move, and a portable charger can ensure that the batteries in your camera remain charged throughout the day.

Even under the most difficult lighting situations, capturing amazing photographs with your camera may be accomplished by using the appropriate settings. When photographing landscapes, setting the aperture to a small number (such as f/16) will help ensure that both the foreground and background are in focus. Additionally, setting the ISO to a low number can assist reduce noise and ensure that your photographs are clear. When photographing wildlife, employing a shutter speed that is very quick (such as 1/500th of a second or faster) might help you freeze the motion of your subjects, which will result in photographs that are very sharp.

When it comes to taking breathtaking photographs in national parks, lighting is one of the most critical considerations that you should give attention to. When it comes to photography, the greatest times of the day are early in the morning and late in the afternoon, because this is when the sun is at its lowest point in the sky and the light is warm and golden. Cloudy days can also give good lighting conditions for photography since the diffuse light can assist decrease harsh shadows and provide a mellow, even glow. This can make cloudy days an excellent time to take pictures.

Finding original points of view and arrangements to photograph in national parks is one of the most effective strategies to get great photographs in these locations. Experiment with a variety of perspectives, focal lengths, and locations of the camera to get photographs that stand out from the rest of the pack. Think about employing leading lines, reflections, and other compositional strategies to create a sense of depth and dimensionality in your photographs. This will help direct the eye of the viewer to the subject of the photograph.

When it comes to taking amazing photographs in national parks, patience is absolutely necessary. It's possible that wildlife is difficult to spot, and the ideal lighting might only be available for a few brief seconds at a time. Prepare yourself to be patient and wait for the perfect opportunity, while also making sure to stop, look about, and appreciate the natural environment that surrounds you. This perseverance and commitment is essential.

When taking photographs in national parks, it is imperative that visitors keep in mind the need to respect the natural surroundings. Stay on approved pathways, don't tramp on plants, and try to have as little of an impact as possible on the surrounding ecosystem by adhering to the Leave No Trace principles. It is important to show proper etiquette when interacting with wild animals and to avoid going too close to them, since this can disrupt their normal behavior and put both you and the animals in danger.

In conclusion, those who are interested in photography will find that national parks provide countless opportunity to take breathtaking photographs of the natural world and to make memories that will last a lifetime. Visitors will be able to make the most of their time in these wonderful locations and capture the essence of the natural beauty that surrounds them if they keep these photography tips and rules in mind while they are there. You may create photographs that genuinely capture the essence of national parks by preparing ahead, acquiring the appropriate equipment, being patient and observant, and approaching the process in this manner. These images will motivate others to appreciate and safeguard these amazing natural riches for future generations.

Chapter IV

Making Plans
for an RV Camping Trip

Creating a budget and saving money for your RV trip

A vacation in an RV is the realization of a long-held fantasy for a lot of people. Many people look forward to the pleasure of having the independence to travel wherever the road may lead them, seeing new places, and learning about other cultures. However, in order to make the most of your time and money during this trip as well as any other journey, it is imperative that you plan ahead and create a budget.

Planning your trip in advance is the first step in creating a budget for your RV vacation and finding ways to cut costs. This requires you to set aside some time to plan out your journey, including the route you will take, the places you will see, and the accommodations you will use. Think about the kinds of things you want to do and how much money each of those things will cost you. Always keep an eye out for offers and discounts, and compare the costs offered by other sellers. If you do your research ahead of time and learn as much as you can about your trip, you'll be in a better position to make educated choices and steer clear of unanticipated costs.

It is essential to your financial well-being to select the appropriate recreational vehicle for your trip. Think on the size and style of recreational vehicle (RV) that you require, as well as whether you will rent or purchase one. If you just plan to use an RV for a short amount of time, renting may be a more cost-effective option for you than buying one; however, purchasing an RV might be a wise investment if you expect to use it for several trips over the course of several years. When purchasing for a recreational vehicle, it is important to search for options that can help you save money in the long run, such as energy-saving appliances and solar panels.

After you have a decent sense of how much your trip will cost, create a budget that takes into account both your income and your outgoing expenses. This can assist you in remaining on track and preventing unnecessary overspending. To begin developing your budget, make a list of all of your anticipated expenditures. These should include things like the cost of food and activities, as well as fuel and camping fees. Next, determine how much money you have available to spend by contrasting your monthly expenditures with your monthly revenue. Make sure you leave some room in your budget for unforeseen costs, such as when you need to get your car fixed or if you have a medical emergency.

On any vacation, the cost of food will likely be one of the most significant expenses. When traveling with a family or a large party, the cost of eating out at restaurants may rapidly add up, especially if you order many courses. Consider preparing some of your own meals in your RV if you want to cut costs. The majority of recreational vehicles (RVs) come furnished with a kitchen that include a refrigerator, stove, and microwave, making it simple to cook your own meals while on the road. In order to reduce food waste, it is important to shop for groceries in bulk at nearby grocery stores or farmer's markets and to prepare meals in advance.

You may cut costs on your RV trip by searching for activities that don't cost much or don't cost anything at all. Children, active duty military personnel, and seniors receive free or subsidized admission to a number of national parks and other attractions across the country. Try to find things to do that are a little off the main road, such as going on a hike, riding a bike, or checking out some of the local museums or historical places. Free forms of entertainment, such as outdoor concerts and festivals, are also available for your enjoyment.

If you intend to do a lot of traveling in your RV, you should look into getting memberships and discount cards so you can save money. There are a variety of groups, like as AAA, Good Sam Club, and Passport America, that provide discounts to RV drivers and owners. You can save money on things like gas, camping fees, and other costs by purchasing one of these clubs. In addition, several clubs provide members with savings on RV insurance, emergency roadside help, and even other services.

On any RV trip, one of the most significant costs will be the fuel. Think about using more fuel-efficient driving techniques, such as lowering your speed and accelerating gradually, in order to cut costs and save money. You may also identify the stations along your route that have the lowest gas prices by using applications such as GasBuddy. One further approach to cut down on expenses related to fuel is to carefully plan out your itinerary. Stay away from unneeded detours and follow the one that will get you to your destination the quickest. You may also think about utilizing alternative fuels, such as biodiesel or propane, both of which have the potential to be less expensive over the course of their use.

Camping in a remote location, also known as boondocking or off-grid camping, is an excellent option to cut costs during your RV vacation. You can save money by not staying at a campground if you park your RV in a distant area and take in the sights of nature without having to contend with other people. People who enjoy camping, fishing, and various other activities in the great outdoors might find this particularly interesting. However, as you are responsible for providing your own water, electricity, and other supplies, boondocking calls for much planning and preparation on your part.

Investing in routine maintenance for your recreational vehicle can, over time, help you realize cost savings. Verify that your recreational vehicle does not have any leaks, perform routine oil changes, and make sure that your tires have the appropriate amount of air in them. Because of this, you may be able to avoid more expensive repairs in the future. You should also be aware of the weight limits of your recreational vehicle (RV), as overloading your vehicle can cause damage and increase the amount of money you spend on fuel.

Finally, if you want to reduce the amount of money you spend on your RV vacation, you might think about traveling outside of the busiest seasons. This may include popular seasons of the year such as holidays and weekends, as well as other times. During these seasons, campers and other attractions may charge higher rates, and it is possible that you may need to make reservations a significant amount of time in advance. Instead, you should think about going during the off-peak seasons, which are characterized by lower pricing and less tourists.

In conclusion, if you want to stick to your spending plan and save money throughout your road trip in your RV, you will need to carefully plan and prepare. You can have a wonderful vacation without breaking the bank if you are strategic about selecting your recreational vehicle (RV), establishing a budget, preparing your own meals, searching for activities that are either free or cost very little money, making use of discount cards and memberships, reducing the amount you spend on fuel, considering boondocking, performing routine maintenance on your RV, and traveling outside of peak travel seasons. Your dream of traveling across the country in an RV might become a reality if you acquire the correct mentality and exercise some inventiveness.

Selecting the ideal season to explore national parks

The scenery that make up our nation's national parks are among the most breathtaking and awe-inspiring on the planet. These parks provide tourists with the opportunity to explore the natural beauty that exists across our world, from the towering peaks of Yosemite to the lush woods of the Great Smoky Mountains. However, it might be difficult to determine the best time of year to travel to national parks and other protected areas.

When organizing a vacation to a national park, the weather is one of the most significant considerations you should give attention to. Some parks are situated in regions that experience climatic conditions that are particularly harsh, such as summers that are swelteringly hot and muggy or winters that are bitterly cold and snowy. Before you start making plans for your vacation, you should do some research on the weather patterns that are typical at your location. This is because the climate can have a significant bearing on the overall quality of your trip.

For instance, if you are thinking about going on vacation to Yellowstone National Park, you should be aware that the park is situated at a somewhat high elevation and that winters there are typically very cold and snowy. The summer months in Yellowstone National Park are ideal for tourists since the temperature is more agreeable and the park is open for activities such as hiking, camping, and other outdoor pursuits. On the other hand, if you're thinking about visiting Zion National Park in Utah any time during the summer, keep in mind that it may get quite crowded and very hot there. The spring and fall seasons offer more pleasant temperatures and less tourists than the summer months do, making them the greatest times to go to Zion National Park.

When arranging a trip to a national park, the number of visitors is another significant aspect to take into consideration. During the busiest times of the year, certain parks can get highly crowded, which can negatively affect the quality of the experience you have there. The natural beauty of the park may be diminished by factors such as lengthy lines, crowded pathways, and restricted parking spaces.

Shoulder season is the period of time between peak season and off-season, and it is a good time to go to national parks if you want to avoid the crowds. Peak season runs from May to September, while off-season is from September to May. You will still be able to appreciate the natural beauty of the park during the shoulder season, but there will be fewer people around. For instance, if you are thinking about going on vacation to Grand Canyon National Park, the best times to go are in the spring or fall because there will be fewer people there and the temperature will be more pleasant.

There is a wide range of plants and animals that may be found in many national parks, including bears, wolves, elk, and other creatures. If you are interested in seeing wildlife, you should schedule your vacation around the time of year when you will have the best chance of observing the creatures in the environment in which they were adapted to live.

For instance, if you're thinking about going on vacation to Denali National Park in Alaska, the greatest time to view grizzly bears is in the late summer and early fall, when salmon are spawning, because that's when the park is most likely to have visitors. During the winter months, when they are more active and visible in Yellowstone National Park, the ideal time to view wolves is during the winter months, so keep that in mind if you are planning a trip there.

The greatest time of year to visit a national park can change depending on the kinds of activities you want to participate in while you're there. If you are interested in hiking, the best time to visit a park may be during the summer months when the trails are open and the temperature is mild because this is typically when the weather is at its most pleasant. On the other hand, if you want to go skiing or snowboarding, the best time to go to a park is probably during the winter months, when the snow is still relatively new and the slopes are accessible.

When organizing a visit to a national park, one last consideration that should not be overlooked is the availability of park services. During the off-season, certain parks may provide fewer services than usual, such as fewer hours of operation at visitor centers or restricted access to certain parts of the park. It is vital to do research on the park services and amenities that are available at the time of year that you want to visit the park so that you can get the most out of your vacation.

As an illustration, if you are thinking about going camping or visiting the visitor center at Acadia National Park in Maine, you should know that both of these facilities are closed during the winter months. However, the park's scenic route is open throughout the entire year and provides visitors with breathtaking vistas of the park's mountains and coastline.

To summarize, planning your trip to a national park during the most appropriate season can have a significant impact on the quality of the time you spend there. You may design a vacation that caters to your interests and satisfies your requirements by taking into account a variety of aspects, including the weather, the number of visitors, the opportunities to watch wildlife, the activities, and the services provided by the park. There is a season that is perfect for you to visit the park, regardless of whether you want to go hiking, watch wildlife, or just take in the natural beauty of the area. You can have an experience at one of the most beautiful national parks in our country that you will remember for the rest of your life if you do your research and plan ahead.

Booking RV campgrounds and making travel plans
When you travel by RV, you have the freedom to go at your own leisure, which is one of the many benefits of doing so. Booking RV

campsites in advance and creating an itinerary are two of the most important things to do if you want to make the most out of your trip, no matter if you are going to drive across the nation or just go away for the weekend.

The first piece of advice I can give regarding booking RV spots is to get a head start. It doesn't take long for popular campgrounds to reach capacity, particularly during high season. If you get a head start on your search, you will have a better chance of locating a location that is suitable for parking your RV. It is recommended that camp sites be reserved at least six months in advance when traveling to popular destinations.

It is crucial to do research on your trip before making any reservations for your campsites. Think about the location, the available amenities, and the local places of interest. To obtain an idea of what to anticipate, look up reviews and suggestions made by people who have previously traveled by RV. This can assist you in finding a campsite that is suitable for your requirements.

It is essential to ensure that you book a campsite that is suitable for your RV when you go to make your reservations. Think on the dimensions and style of your recreational vehicle, as well as the conveniences you'd like most, such as water, electric, and sewage hookups. It's possible that some campgrounds offer more amenities than others, so it's important to select a location that's suitable for your requirements.

It is highly recommended that you make your reservations for campsites directly with the campground. This will assist you avoid having to pay any additional fees and will guarantee the safety of your reservation. Many campgrounds now offer online reservations, which campers will find to be more convenient and user-friendly than traditional methods.

Consider signing up for a discount program like the Good Sam Club or Passport America if you want to do a lot of driving in your recreational vehicle. These programs may provide savings on campsites, in addition to savings on other services, such as insurance for recreational vehicles and roadside assistance.

Taking into account your interests is the first thing you should do while organizing your schedule. Are you interested in going fishing, hiking, or discovering the local points of interest? If you know what you want to accomplish on your trip, it will be easier to plan your route and select your campsites.

After identifying your areas of interest, the next step is to plan out your path. Think on how far apart your camping spots are, as well as how much time it will take you to get from one to the other. Be sure to take into account any stops along the journey that you might like to make, whether they be at scenic overlooks or local attractions.

It is essential to maintain a flexible mindset when organizing your agenda. On the road, unanticipated occurrences like traffic jams or road closures can take place at any time. You should be ready to make adjustments to your plan if they become necessary, and you should give some thought to leaving some open time in your agenda to provide room for impromptu activities.

Make sure to do some research on the local attractions before you start planning your agenda. Some of the many possible attractions are national parks, museums, and historical places. These are only a few instances of the many possibilities. You may save money on admission prices by looking for discounts or coupons that will help you save money.

You may cut costs and avoid making unneeded stops along the trip if you plan your meals in advance and prepare them in advance. You might want to bring a cooler with some snacks and drinks with you, and you should base your meal planning on the facilities that are offered at the campsites you choose.

It is essential to take into account the weather whenever you are organizing your schedule. specific periods of the year, such as in the fall when the leaves change color or in the spring when the flowers are in bloom, may be more enjoyable for visiting specific locations than other times of the year. Be sure to check the weather forecast for each location that you will be visiting along your journey. This will allow you to pack accordingly and ensure that you are ready for any kind of weather.

It is imperative that you remember your safety while you are organizing your itinerary. Always adhere to the regulations and norms for road safety, and stay alert for any potential dangers that may be along your journey. When going camping, it is essential to take the required safety precautions, such as locking up your recreational vehicle and maintaining a first aid kit at all times.

Finally, when you are organizing the details of your itinerary, don't forget to factor in time for rest stops along the road. Driving for extended periods of time can be exhausting; taking regular pauses will help you avoid falling asleep behind the wheel and keep your mind sharp. Think about pulling over at rest stops or scenic overlooks so that you may stretch your legs and take in the scenery.

To summarize, if you want to get the most out of your RV journey, it is critical to make reservations for RV campgrounds and to create an itinerary. You can locate the ideal parking area for your RV if you get a head start, do some research on your trip, pick the correct kind of campsite, make your reservation directly with the campground, and take advantage of any discount programs they may provide. When you are organizing your schedule, it is important to keep the following things in mind: your interests; creating a route; being flexible; researching local sites; preparing meals; keeping an eye on the weather; remaining safe; and taking breaks. You may enjoy a trip in your RV that you will never forget if you follow these suggestions and guidelines.

Safety recommendations for RV camping in national parks

Camping in a recreational vehicle at one of our nation's national parks is one of the best ways to get out into nature and appreciate the natural beauty of our world. However, in order to secure your safety when camping, it is essential to take the necessary precautions.

It is imperative that you familiarize yourself with the policies and guidelines of the national park in which you plan to camp in a recreational vehicle. Each national park is governed by its own unique set of regulations, the purpose of which is to safeguard both visitors and the natural environment. Be careful to familiarize yourself with the park's laws and regulations ahead of time and adhere to them throughout your stay there.

When camping in a recreational vehicle within of a national park, it is important to make preparations ahead of time. Think about the upcoming weather, the topography, and everything else that can affect your ability to stay safe. You need to be sure that you have all of the necessary equipment and materials for your journey, such as a first aid kit, maps, and a dependable method of contact.

When RV camping in a national park, picking the correct spot to park your vehicle is one of the most important things you can do to ensure your safety. Look for camping areas that are well lit, have easy access to water and other amenities, and are situated far away from potential dangers such as steep cliffs and swift-moving water. Steer clear of campgrounds that are too near to other RVs or that are located in congested regions.

Maintaining your sense of security while camping can be facilitated by properly securing your RV. When you leave your RV, make sure to lock all of the doors and windows, and keep expensive objects hidden from view. As a preventative measure against theft, you might think about making an investment in security gadgets such as a GPS tracker or alarm system.

There is a wide range of wildlife that calls a number of our nation's national parks home, including bears, cougars, and other potentially hazardous species. It is essential to be aware of the local wildlife and to take the necessary safety measures to prevent any unwanted interactions. Bear-resistant containers should be used for storing food and garbage, and you should maintain a respectful distance from any wild animals you come across.

When camping in recreational vehicles inside national parks, it is essential to practice fire prevention. Make sure you are aware with the fire rules of the park, and then make sure you follow those regulations. Your recreational vehicle (RV) should always have a fire extinguisher, and you should know how to use it. Before you walk away from the campfire and leave it alone, make sure it has been properly extinguished.

Because unexpected events might take place at any time, it is critical to always be ready. Always have a first aid kit on you, and be sure you are familiar of how to use it. Carry one with you wherever you go. In the event of a medical or other urgent situation, you should be prepared with a game plan and know the location of the closest hospital or emergency services.

Leave No Trace is a collection of guiding principles developed with the intention of reducing the negative effects of human activity on the natural world. Leave No Trace is a set of rules that, when followed, can help protect both the natural beauty of national parks and your personal safety. Keep in mind that you are responsible for packing out all waste, staying on trails that have been designated for that purpose, and avoiding causing any damage to the surrounding plants.

When RV camping in national parks, showing consideration for the safety of fellow campers is one way to reduce your risk of injury. Maintain a low volume of noise during designated "quiet hours," and try not to disturb your fellow campers with bright lights or loud music. Maintain a clean and orderly campsite while showing consideration for other campers' right to personal space and privacy.

Keeping in contact with others when RV camping in national parks can help you avoid potential dangers. Make certain that you have a dependable method of communication on hand, such as a mobile phone or a satellite phone. Share your travel plans and estimated time of return with a friend or family member, and make sure to check in with them frequently.

In conclusion, camping in national parks with recreational vehicles can be a wonderful way to take in the splendor of the natural world. Nevertheless, it is necessary to use caution in order to protect your well-being. You can have a fun and safe RV camping trip in a national park by being familiar with the rules and regulations, planning ahead, selecting the appropriate campsite, securing your RV, being aware of wildlife, practicing fire safety, being prepared for emergencies, practicing the principles of Leave No Trace, respecting other campers, and staying connected. If you keep these safety recommendations in mind, you will be able to appreciate the natural beauty of our world without putting your safety at risk.

Conclusion

Recap of the benefits of RV camping in national parks

Camping in recreational vehicles (RVs) in national parks is a well-liked and enjoyable method to take in the breathtaking scenery of our planet. National parks give tourists the opportunity to enjoy the natural beauties of the area they are visiting. This might range from the towering peaks of Yosemite to the lush woods of the Great Smoky Mountains.

The lower cost of RV camping in national parks is one of the most significant advantages of doing so. Camping in a recreational vehicle, as opposed to staying in a hotel or renting a house for a holiday, can be much more affordable. RVs provide a number of the same conveniences that are available in hotel rooms, such as a bed, a bathroom, and a kitchen, but at a significantly lower cost. You can save even more money by camping in one of the nation's many national parks, many of which provide either subsidized or free sites for campers.

Another advantage of camping in national parks with an RV is the flexibility it offers. Traveling in an RV gives you the freedom to go at your own leisure and discover the park at your own convenience. You are free to stay for as long or as little as you wish, and you can move on to a new campground whenever you feel the need. Because of this flexibility, you will be able to make the most of your trip and take in the breathtaking scenery of the park without feeling as though you are pressed for time.

When you stay in a hotel or a vacation rental, you miss out on the opportunity to interact with nature in ways that are available when you camp in a recreational vehicle in a national park. You can fall asleep to the sight of the stars, wake up to the sound of birds chirping, and go on hikes through natural areas that have not been disturbed. This connection with nature has the potential to be a refreshing and invigorating experience, as well as one that can teach you to appreciate the stunning natural beauty of our planet.

Hiking, fishing, paddling a kayak, and looking at wild animals are just few of the many outdoor pursuits that may be enjoyed in national parks. Camping in an RV gives you the freedom to participate in these activities at your own speed and according to your own schedule. In addition, many national parks include activities and excursions given by park rangers, which can help you learn more about the area as well as its history.

Camping with recreational vehicles within national parks is a fun and family-friendly activity. Because recreational vehicles (RVs) come equipped with a kitchen and a bathroom, much like a regular house, taking a trip with children may be done in a much more relaxed manner. In addition, national parks provide a wide range of activities that are appropriate for people of all ages, such as hiking, watching wildlife, and stargazing.

It's possible to make new friends when camping in national parks with your RV. You can meet other campers and share stories and experiences with them in the common spaces that many campsites provide. These communal areas typically consist of fire pits and picnic tables. In addition, a large number of national parks provide visitors with the opportunity to participate in activities that are led by park rangers and to go on tours that are led by park rangers. These are both excellent ways to meet other tourists and to gain more knowledge about the area.

Camping in national parks with a recreational vehicle can be a really pleasant experience. RV camping gives you the opportunity to relax and reenergize because you are immersed in natural settings and removed from the stresses of everyday life. You can take a leisurely stroll, sit by the fire, or read a book by the fire. This type of relaxation may be an experience that is both invigorating and restorative, and it can also help you de-stress and recharge your batteries.

An educational opportunity may be found while camping in a recreational vehicle in a national park. You may find a variety of information about the natural world in national parks, and many of them also provide activities and tours given by park rangers, which can help you learn more about the park itself and its history. In addition, going camping in an RV may teach you valuable skills such as how to cook outdoors, how to navigate wilderness areas, and how to put the "Leave No Trace" ideals into practice.

In conclusion, camping in national parks in an RV offers a wide variety of advantages, including the advantages of being affordable, educational, and relaxing. RV camping in national parks may be an enriching and satisfying experience since it provides campers with the opportunity to interact with nature, take part in a variety of outdoor pursuits, meet new people, and gain new knowledge about the natural world. RV camping in national parks offers something for everyone, whether you're a family looking for a vacation that is both fun and economical, an outdoor enthusiast searching for excitement and a connection with nature, or just someone looking for a way to unwind and relax. It is not surprising that RV camping in national parks is such a popular activity given the abundance of advantages associated with doing so. Why not start planning your very own RV camping trip right now and see the natural wonders and breathtaking scenery of our national parks for yourself?

Final thoughts and recommendations

Camping in a recreational vehicle within one of our nation's national parks is one of the most spectacular ways to take in the breathtaking scenery of the earth. National parks provide visitors with the opportunity to connect with nature and explore some of the most breathtaking environments in the world. These parks are located all throughout the United States, ranging from the towering peaks of the Rocky Mountains to the lush forests of the Pacific Northwest.

When camping in national parks with an RV, one of the most essential pieces of advice is to make advance preparations. Campsites in national parks can fill up rapidly, particularly during the busiest times of the year, so visitors should plan accordingly. You can make sure that you will have a place to park your RV and that you will be able to enjoy the park by making preparations in advance and reserving campsites.

Being well-prepared is another essential piece of advice for those who camp in recreational vehicles in national parks. Because national parks are often located in isolated areas, it is imperative that visitors come prepared with the necessary equipment and supplies in order to travel safely and in comfort. Make sure you bring along some basic medical supplies, a lot of water, and a dependable method of communication such as a cell phone or a satellite phone.

The Leave No Trace principles are a collection of recommendations that were developed to assist in reducing the negative effects that human activities can have on the natural world. The Leave No Trace principles can help you stay safe while also contributing to the preservation of the natural beauty that national parks are known for. Keep in mind that you are responsible for packing out all waste, staying on trails that have been designated for that purpose, and avoiding causing any damage to the surrounding plants.

There is a wide range of animals that call national parks their home, therefore it is essential to give them their space and refrain from disturbing them in any way. Be cautious to put your food and waste in containers that are bear-proof, and always maintain a safe distance from any wild animals you come across. Never approach wild animals or feed them, as this puts both you and the animals in a potentially dangerous situation.

Respect for one's fellow campers is essential when traveling through national parks in recreational vehicles. Maintain a low volume of noise during designated "quiet hours," and try not to disturb your fellow campers with bright lights or loud music. Maintain a clean and orderly campsite while showing consideration for other campers' right to personal space and privacy.

There are a number of national parks that provide activities and tours conducted by rangers, and participating in them can be an excellent opportunity to learn more about the park and its past. Participating in these activities is not only fun, but also a fantastic way to meet fellow tourists and compare travel stories. Check the schedule of events that will be held at the park and make the most of the opportunities that will be presented to you.

If you want to make RV camping in national parks a regular part of your vacation routine, you might think about joining a discount program like the Good Sam Club or Passport America. These programs may provide savings on campsites, in addition to savings on other services, such as insurance for recreational vehicles and roadside assistance.

It is crucial to do research about your destination before departing on your RV camping trip. Think about the location, the available amenities, and the local places of interest. To obtain an idea of what to anticipate, look up reviews and suggestions made by people who have previously traveled by RV. This might make it easier for you to select a campground that is suitable for your requirements and ensure that you have a wonderful trip.

When RV camping in national parks, your recreational vehicle serves as your home away from home; therefore, it is essential to maintain its condition. It is imperative that you keep your RV clean and well-maintained at all times, as well as do routine maintenance and inspections on it. This will help ensure that your RV is in good shape and able to maintain your comfort throughout the journey.

Having a good time and making the most of the experience is, without a doubt, the single most essential piece of advice regarding RV camping in national parks. RV camping provides a one-of-a-kind and enriching perspective on America's national parks, which are home to some of the world's most breathtaking scenery. RV camping in national parks provides an opportunity to interact with nature and make experiences that will last a lifetime. This can take the form of activities such as taking a hike through untouched wilderness, gazing at the stars at night, or telling stories to other campers around a campfire.

In conclusion, camping in a recreational vehicle within a national park can be an amazing and fulfilling experience. You can have a safe, enjoyable, and memorable RV camping trip in a national park if you plan ahead, are prepared, adhere to the principles of Leave No Trace, show respect for wildlife and other campers, take advantage of ranger-led activities, join discount programs, do research on your destination, take care of your RV, and have fun. It is not surprising that RV camping in national parks is such a well-liked pastime given the abundance of advantages and chances that it presents.

Resources for planning your RV camping trip

Organizing a camping vacation in a recreational vehicle can be a fun and gratifying experience. There are numerous tools available that can assist you in planning your trip and making the most of your experience, regardless of whether you are an experienced RV camper or embarking on your first big adventure.

National Park Service Website

The website of the National Park Service is a vital tool to have on hand if you want to camp in a recreational vehicle within a national park. The website provides information on a variety of topics, including things like park fees, campgrounds, events, and more. You can also acquire information regarding the rules and regulations of the park, as well as download brochures and maps. Because the website is updated on a regular basis, it is important that you revisit it on a regular basis in order to obtain the most recent information.

Recreation.gov

Campsites at national parks and other public lands can be reserved through the website Recreation.gov. This website is also available for other public properties. You can search for available campsites online, narrowing your results by location, date, and amenities, and then reserve a spot for yourself. In addition to this, the website provides links to other helpful resources and details on the various events and activities that take place in the parks.

Reserve America

Another website that allows you to reserve campsites in national parks and other public lands is called Reserve America. You can search for available campsites online, narrowing your results by location, date, and amenities, and then reserve a spot for yourself. In addition to this, the website provides links to other helpful resources and details on the various events and activities that take place in the parks.

Good Sam Club

RV owners can join the Good Sam Club, which is an organization dedicated to their needs. Members are entitled to savings on campgrounds, RV insurance, and other services, in addition to having access to many tools and information for vacation planning. The club also provides its members with access to a community of other individuals who are interested in RVing and a nationwide network of RV parks and campgrounds.

RV Trip Wizard

RV Trip Wizard is a website as well as an app that enables you to organize every step of your camping vacation using your recreational vehicle. You can enter your starting point and your destination on the website, and it will build a personalized route for you that takes into account elements such as the amount of mileage traveled, the cost of fuel, and the availability of camping spots. You also have the option of including several stops and sites of interest along the route.

RV Park Reviews

RV Park Reviews is a website that provides users with the ability to browse reviews and ratings of RV parks and campgrounds located all across the United States. You can search for campgrounds based on their location, and then read reviews written by other RVers about their experiences there. Additionally, the website provides information on the available amenities, as well as pricing and other pertinent particulars.

AllStays

Both a website and an app, AllStays provides users with a comprehensive database of RV parks and campgrounds located all across the United States. You are able to search for parks based on their locations, and obtain information on their amenities, fees, and other specifics. Additionally, the program provides offline maps in addition to other helpful tools for RV camping.

AAA

AAA is a membership-based organization that provides its members with a variety of benefits, including savings on travel and emergency roadside help. In addition, AAA provides tools and resources for vacation planning, such as path routing, hotel bookings, and travel insurance services. The AAA is a great website that may help you plan your itinerary and earn discounts on travel-related charges if you are going to be camping in an RV.

RVillage

RVillage is a social networking platform specifically designed for those who travel by RV. You are able to connect with other RVers through the website and app, as well as share information and resources with one another and receive recommendations for RV parks and campgrounds. RVillage additionally provides resources for vacation planning, such as route mapping and reservations for camping spots.

State Tourism Websites

If you want to go camping in a recreational vehicle (RV) in a certain state, the tourist website for that state can be a helpful resource for arranging your vacation. The tourist websites of individual states provide information on the state's various resources, including campgrounds, parks, attractions, and other areas of interest. You are also able to obtain information on driving routes, the weather, and other relevant information. Some state tourism websites even provide tools and resources for trip planning, such as interactive maps and suggested itineraries, to help travelers get the most out of their vacations.

In conclusion, preparing for a camping vacation in an RV may be an experience that is both exciting and fulfilling. You may increase the likelihood that your vacation will be safe, pleasurable, and memorable if you make use of these information and tools. There are many tools available to assist you in planning your journey and making the most of your experience. These resources range from websites and reservation systems for national parks to social networking platforms and RV clubs. Why not start arranging your own RV camping trip right now and discover the beauty and wonder of our nation's public lands and national parks?

Thank you for buying and reading/listening to our book. If you found this book useful/helpful please take a few minutes and leave a review on Amazon.com or Audible.com (if you bought the audio version).

9 781088 194041